TEACHING LITERATURE TO ADOLESCENTS: NOVELS

ALAN B. HOWES
University of Michigan

TEACHING

LITERATURE

TO

ADOLESCENTS

SCOTT, FORESMAN AND COMPANY   Glenview, Illinois   London

PN
3385
.H68

The author wishes to thank those who have given permission to reprint the following:
Excerpts from **A Different Drummer** by William Melvin Kelley. Copyright © 1962 by William Melvin Kelley. Reprinted by permission of Doubleday & Company, Inc., and William Morris Agency, Inc. on behalf of the author. Material from screenplay **The Adventures of Huckleberry Finn** supplied by Metro-Goldwyn-Mayer Inc., © 1939 Loew's Incorporated, copyright renewed 1966 by Metro-Goldwyn-Mayer Inc. Reprinted by permission. An excerpt from **A Farewell to Arms** by Ernest Hemingway. Reprinted by permission of Charles Scribner's Sons and Jonathan Cape Ltd. Copyright 1929 Charles Scribner's Sons; renewal copyright © 1957 Ernest Hemingway. Chapters 31 and 32 from **The True Adventures of Huckleberry Finn,** told by John Seelye (Evanston: Northwestern University Press, 1970). Reprinted by permission. An excerpt from **Beetlecreek** by William Demby. Reprinted by permission of Curtis Brown, Ltd. Copyright, 1950, by William Demby. Excerpts from pp. 69–71, 48, 159–160, 172 (as scattered quotes) from **Black Boy** (hardbound edition) by Richard Wright. Copyright 1937, 1942, 1944, 1945 by Richard Wright. Reprinted by permission of Harper & Row, Publishers, Inc., Mrs. Ellen Wright, and Jonathan Cape Ltd. Excerpts from **Black Like Me** by John H. Griffin. Copyright © 1960, 1961 by John Howard Griffin. Reprinted by permission of the publisher, Houghton Mifflin Company, and the author. An excerpt from **Harvey's Hideout** by Russell Hoban, by permission of Parents' Magazine Press. Excerpts from **High School English Instruction Today,** by James R. Squire and Roger K. Applebee, Appleton-Century-Crofts, 1968, pp. 109, 120. Excerpts from **Hurt, Baby, Hurt,** by William Walter Scott, III, An Arbor: New Ghetto Press, 1970, pp. 67—69, 158—159. Excerpt reprinted from **Madame Bovary,** Norton Critical Edition, by Gustave Flaubert. Edited with a substantially new translation by Paul de Man. By permission of W. W. Norton & Company, Inc. Copyright © 1965 by W. W. Norton & Company, Inc. Excerpts from **Manchild in the Promised Land,** by Claude Brown. Reprinted with permission of The Macmillan Company, and Jonathan Cape Ltd. Copyright © 1965 by Claude Brown. Excerpts from **Of Mice and Men** (novel and play versions) by John Steinbeck. Copyright 1937, copyright © renewed 1965 by John Steinbeck. All rights reserved. Reprinted by permission of The Viking Press, Inc., and McIntosh & Otis, Inc. Excerpts from **"Four Kinds of Reading,"** in *Speaking of Books,* by Donald Hall, *New York Times Book Review,* January 26, 1969, pp. 2, 30. © 1959 by The New York Times Company. Reprinted by permission. Adaptation from pages 124–126 of **The Street,** by Ann Petry. Copyright, 1946, by Ann Petry. Reprinted by permission of the publisher, Houghton Mifflin Company. Excerpt from **I Know Why the Caged Bird Sings,** by Maya Angelou. Copyright © 1969 by Maya Angelou. Reprinted by permission of Random House, Inc.

Preface

"The only obligation to which in advance we may hold a novel," Henry James once said, "is that it be interesting" *(The Art of Fiction).* Robert Louis Stevenson, on the other hand, thought that works of fiction were not only interesting but also "the most influential books." They "clarify the lessons of life," he said, and "show us the web of experience" *(Books Which Have Influenced Me).* The teacher—especially the teacher of adolescents—may well hesitate between these two attitudes, wondering where to put the emphasis. Should he teach works of fiction primarily as "interesting" or "exciting" stories, or should he teach them mainly as "significant" books which can change or develop attitudes in adolescents? This book implies that the dilemma described above is to a large degree a false one, since the "significant" and the "interesting" must be seen as inextricably joined if fiction is to be taught successfully. Oscar Wilde was right in one sense when he asserted that "the only real people are the people who never existed" *(The Decay of Lying),* for the characters of a novelist can achieve both an intensity and a significance larger than the life around us.

Teaching Literature to Adolescents: Novels tries to help teachers and teachers-to-be find ways to lead students to an appreciation of that intensity and that significance. It provides a theoretical rationale which should be useful for either experienced or prospective teachers and suggests ways in which theory can be translated into classroom practice. It concentrates on such questions as these: How can teachers make the reading of fiction a different experience from the reading of drama? What critical tools and concepts about fiction should inform the approaches that a teacher takes to specific works? How should the presentation of a novel differ at different levels (using *Huckleberry Finn* as an example)? How can teachers make more use of literature by black writers? Finally, how can the activities of each student be geared to his own talent and interest at the same time that the class as a group shares certain common experiences? In the course of discussing these and similar questions, I have treated, at varying lengths, a wide diversity of narrative works, ranging from *Beowulf* to *King Kong,* from *Robinson Crusoe* to *Henderson the Rain King.* (For the student or teacher wishing to read more than my selected quotations from any of these works, but who is unable to obtain the edition cited in the footnote, I have given chapter or section as well as page numbers and have included a Bibliography of suggested paperback editions.)

I am especially grateful to the distinguished novelists who consented to "interviews." Alan Paton, John Knowles, and Conrad Richter represent more than one generation and more than one country, but they have in common the achievement of winning devoted adolescent as well as adult readers. It is poignant that the questions for the interview should be the last thing that Conrad Richter worked on before his death, but it is also peculiarly fitting, since *The Light in the Forest* in particular has fascinated so many teen-agers as well as adults.

I am happy to record other debts. Miss Jean Reynolds, Language Arts Coordinator for the Ann Arbor Public Schools, and Stephen Dunning, my colleague and collaborator in this series of books on teaching literature to adolescents, have both read the entire manuscript and made constructive suggestions. My colleague Darwin T. Turner read an early draft of Part Four and performed the invaluable service of making me sufficiently dissatisfied with it to revise and expand that section into its present form, as well as giving me specific advice about ways in which literature by black writers could be used. The editorial staff at Scott, Foresman, and especially Carol Embury, Barbara Putta, and Pat Lafferty, have provided various kinds of valuable assistance. Finally, my wife, Lidie, has been typist, editor, critic, and willing audience by turns: each role has been enormously helpful.

Alan B. Howes
Ann Arbor, Michigan
June 1, 1971

Contents

TEACHING LITERATURE TO ADOLESCENTS: NOVELS

PART ONE

Teaching Plays and Novels

Some Distinctions

Plays and novels offer many of the same advantages to the teacher. Both tell a story—and can give students the excitement of finding out what characters will do next. Both present well-developed characters—and can give students the rewards of identification or rejection, of agreement or disagreement with idea and act. Both may seem closer to the lives of junior and senior high school students than the often more philosophic statements of poetry they read, or the seemingly more remote intellectual concerns of the essay. Both can lead the student to enter another world—and if that world is made to come alive for students, it is both exciting and meaningful.

The world of the novel is in some ways easier to enter than the world of the play. Written to be read rather than to be produced, the novel makes fewer demands upon the reader, since action, gesture, and movement are apt to be explicitly described rather than merely implied or left to the imagination, as they often are in the text of a play. The novelist shapes his tale as he tells it, often adding the kind of explicit comment that the dramatist, with his seemingly more objective point of view, is barred from making even in stage directions. The reader is often left in less doubt about motive and meaning in a novel than in a play. From one point of view, the novel may be considered a kind of expanded play, with fuller stage directions and authorial comment added.

Yet the student who comes to regard play and novel as virtually equivalent forms—one being merely more fully developed than the other—has been cheated of the full appreciation of the unique literary experience that each form can offer. The teacher must avoid the temptation, stemming from the similarities of the two forms, to ignore their differences and teach them both as "stories" to be considered in exactly the same way. He should be aware of the special insights and satisfactions that may come from the study of each form and the differences in approach that make these insights and satisfactions possible.

Too often a particular novel or play is viewed as having an arbitrarily chosen form expressing a theme which might have been as well expressed in the other form. Attempts to turn plays into novels—or novels into plays or films—demonstrate the unsoundness of this view. The novelists whose remarks appear in the interviews in Part Five are unanimous in their feeling that neither play nor film is usually equivalent to the novel. Conrad Richter believes that often "reputable novels were turned into films that bore little resemblance to the story or credibility of the original work." John Knowles thinks that in spite of "some good film portrayals," they provide only "the palest shadow of what we get in the novel." Alan Paton was "quite numbed" to see the stage adaptation of *Cry, the Beloved Country,* though he finally "was able to see it as a work of art existing in its own right." Translation from one form to the other is usually unsatisfactory, somehow less rich than the original. And this fact should lead us as teachers to try to teach each form for its own peculiar pleasures and effects. Even where the same theme may emerge from a play and a novel, the way in which it emerges is significant for students' understanding and appreciation, since a work of literature provides a total experience, not a neatly summarizable theme, point, or moral.

Of Mice and Men

Some of the distinctions between drama and novel can perhaps be hinted at by looking at a work that has two versions by the same author, one in dramatic and one in fictional form. John Steinbeck's *Of Mice and Men* is a good test case, since there is a minimum of difference between the two versions—Steinbeck's novel is more than usually rich in dialogue for a novel, and the pattern of action for his play is perhaps closer to the typical pattern of action for a novel than is that of most plays. Both versions present the tragedy of George and Lennie, two migrant workers who hope someday to buy a place of their own. Lennie, mentally retarded, is phenomenally strong; he is also irresistibly attracted to soft, small things like mice and puppies, which he unintentionally crushes and kills when he pets them. George, tied down and yet saved from aimless drifting by the responsibility of looking after Lennie, is constantly fearful of what Lennie may do as the pair move from one migratory farm job to another. In the end the daughter-in-law of their present boss encourages Lennie to stroke her hair but becomes frightened and tries to get free from his iron grip. Lennie, terrified and bewildered, kills her with his powerful hands. George then shoots Lennie before the other farmhands can hunt him down in a posse.

In both play and novel the action is the same, and almost all of the dialogue of the play is to be found in the novel. The six chapters of the novel are made into three acts (six scenes) for the play. Even the stage directions for the play attempt to reproduce the scene of the novel and much of the authorial comment on how characters speak and act. Yet there are significant, though seemingly minor, differences between the two versions, and these differences hint at some of the inevitable distinctions between play and novel that affect our perception of characters and understanding of theme in each form.

The use of exposition. One of the most obvious contrasts between the two versions, demonstrating Steinbeck's affinity for the novel form, occurs in the scene in which we are introduced to the character of Slim. Here is the way Steinbeck does it in the novel:

A tall man stood in the doorway. He held a crushed Stetson hat under his arm while he combed his long, black, damp hair straight back. Like the others he wore blue jeans and a short denim jacket. When he had finished combing his hair he moved into the room, and he moved with a majesty only achieved by royalty and master craftsmen. He was a jerkline skinner, the prince of the ranch, capable of driving ten, sixteen, even twenty mules with a single line to the leaders. He was capable of killing a fly on the wheeler's butt with a bull whip without touching the mule. There was a gravity in his manner and a quiet so profound that all talk stopped when he spoke. His authority was so great that his word was taken on any subject, be it politics or love. This was Slim, the jerkline skinner. His hatchet face was ageless. He might have been thirty-five or fifty. His ear heard more than was said to him, and his slow speech had overtones not of thought, but of understanding beyond thought. His hands, large and lean, were as delicate in their action as those of a temple dancer.

He smoothed out his crushed hat, creased it in the middle and put it on. He looked kindly at the two in the bunk house.

"It's brighter'n a bitch outside," he said gently. "Can't hardly
see nothing in here. You the new guys?"

"Just come," said George.

"Gonna buck barley?"

"That's what the boss says."

Slim sat down on a box across the table from George. He
studied the solitaire hand that was upside down to him. "Hope
you get on my team," he said. His voice was very gentle. "I
gotta pair of punks on my team that don't know a barley bag
from a blue ball. . . ."[1]

Here is the way Steinbeck writes the same scene for the dramatic
version:

> SLIM. *(Enters C. He is a tall, dark man in blue-jeans and
> short denim jacket. Carries a crushed Stetson hat under his arm
> and combs his long dark damp hair straight back. Stands and
> moves with a kind of majesty. Finishes combing his hair.
> Smooths out his crushed hat, creases it in the middle and puts it
> on. In a gentle voice.)* It's brighter'n a bitch outside. Can't hard-
> ly see nothing in here. You the new guys?
>
> GEORGE. Just come.
>
> SLIM. Goin' to buck barley?
>
> GEORGE. That's what the boss says.
>
> SLIM. Hope you get on my team.
>
> GEORGE. Boss said we'd go with a jerk-line skinner named
> Slim.
>
> SLIM. That's me.
>
> GEORGE. You a jerk-line skinner?
>
> SLIM. *(In self-disparagement.)* I can snap 'em around a little.
>
> GEORGE. *(Terribly impressed.)* That kinda makes you Jesus
> Christ on this ranch, don't it?
>
> SLIM. *(Obviously pleased.)* Oh, nuts!
>
> GEORGE. *(Chuckles.)* Like the man says, "The boss tells you
> what to do. But if you want to know how to do it, you got to
> ask the mule skinner." The man says any guy that can drive
> twelve Arizona jack rabbits with a jerk line can fall in a toilet
> and come up with a mince pie under each arm.
>
> SLIM. *(Laughing.)* Well, I hope you get on my team. I got a
> pair of punks that don't know a barley bag from a blue
> ball. . . .[2]

1. John Steinbeck, *Of Mice and Men* (New York: The Viking Press, 1965), Ch. 2, pp. 36–37.
2. John Steinbeck, *Of Mice and Men,* Dramatic version (New York: Dramatists Play Service, Inc.,
1964), p. 28.

The difference between the two passages does not merely lie in the fact that Steinbeck reduced the narrative exposition of the novel by two thirds when he wrote stage directions for the dramatic version, though this loss is significant in itself. More important, we gain a more finished portrait of Slim in the novel version, partly because the most important elements in his character are easier for a narrator to tell us about than for a dramatist to demonstrate on stage. In the dramatic version George's awed comments are about jerk-line skinners in general, while in the novel the narrator can present Slim both as type and as individual, for though all jerk-line skinners presumably have some of Slim's talents, surely not all of them speak in a manner with "overtones not of thought, but of understanding beyond thought." The speeches in the play provide a somewhat awkward piece of necessary exposition; the authorial comment in the novel is natural and appropriate.

The use of action. Though the events remain almost the same in the two versions, one can see how minor changes in the action have been dictated by the need of the play for compression or heightening of dramatic scenes, and the contrasting tendency of the novel toward a looser, more expanded form. Act II, scene 2 of the play, for example, focuses on the hope that George and Lennie have for a place of their own and on the possible threats to that hope. It is Saturday night and George has gone with the other men to a nearby town for a drink or two at Miss Susy's, although he has decided not to spend any money for a girl there. He returns early, explaining why he didn't even want to spend money for a drink: "I'm jus' gonna set out a dime and a nickel for a shot an' I think what a hell of a lot of bulk carrot seed you can get for fifteen cents."[3] He finds Lennie talking to Candy, the old man who cleans the bunkhouse, and Crooks, the Negro stable hand, in the latter's room in the barn. Candy has previously been admitted to a place in George and Lennie's secret plans for buying a place of their own and he and Lennie talk about their plans. Crooks has just offered to work for them for nothing if he is allowed to join the project, when George enters. A few moments later Curley's wife (the boss' daughter-in-law) enters, ostensibly to ask Crooks a question. The men, sensing trouble, try to get her to leave, but she is defiant and insults them by calling them "lousy bindle bums." Candy then boasts: "You don't know we got our own ranch to go to an' our own house an' fruit trees. An' we got friends. . . . Maybe they was a time when we didn't have nothing, but that ain't so no more."[4] Curley's wife doesn't really believe him; she is interested only in

3. *Ibid.,* p. 54.
4. *Ibid.,* p. 55.

finding out what happened to Curley's hand. (Lennie, goaded into a fight by Curley's unprovoked attack, had crushed it with his great strength, but Curley had been reassured that if he kept silent about the details of his injury, the others would.) Curley's wife finally gathers that Lennie is responsible; she is being ejected by George when the boss appears in the doorway as the scene ends. In this scene the dramatic conflicts have all centered around threats to George and Lennie's plans for a place of their own: the possibilities of disclosure of the plans to people who could thwart or destroy them have provided the excitement of the scene.

In the corresponding section of the novel, Chapter Four, our attention is focused on the Negro Crooks and his loneliness in a world of white men, paralleled by Candy's loneliness as an old man in a world of younger men. George does not return until the very end of the scene. In the meantime Curley's wife has entered just after Crooks has made his offer to Candy and Lennie to join the project for a place of their own. Crooks tries to get Curley's wife to leave, telling her that if she doesn't, he will ask the boss never to let her come in the barn. She threatens him: "'Listen, Nigger,' she said, 'You know what I can do to you if you open your trap? . . . I could get you strung up on a tree so easy it ain't even funny.'" Candy objects that he and Lennie would tell about the frame-up, but she says, "Nobody'd listen to you," and Candy is forced to agree.[5] After she has left, George enters, and at the end of the scene Crooks, having "retired into the terrible protective dignity of the Negro" during the scene and "reduced himself to nothing . . . [with] no personality,"[6] retracts his offer to work for the other men if they buy a place of their own. This chapter has been in effect Crooks' chapter, with its focus on the tragedy of the loss of his bid for a place in George and Lennie's plans. In the play, the focus has remained on George and Lennie, and the threats of Curley's wife to Crooks have been eliminated.

A similar change in focus for the purpose of dramatic heightening of conflict may be seen in Act III, scene 2 of the play, as contrasted with Chaper Six of the novel. In both, after killing Curley's wife, Lennie has gone back to the river bank of the opening scene, as George had instructed him to do in case of trouble. George, knowing where to find Lennie, has headed there, while the other ranch hands have formed a posse to look for Lennie. In the novel version George finds Lennie and, while talking about the place they hope to have someday, shoots him in the back of the head before the posse arrives. In the dramatic version, George runs ahead of the other men and finds

5. Steinbeck, *Of Mice and Men,* Novel version, Ch. 4, pp. 88–89.
6. *Ibid.,* Ch. 4, pp. 86–89.

Lennie but makes him hide in the bulrushes just as the others arrive. Slim, sensing from George's expression that Lennie is near, gets the men to spread out and move off to look in other directions so that George can do what must be done. He remains a moment after the others have gone and asks George if he wants him to go away. George nods and there is a moment of communion between the two men as Slim exits. George then shoots Lennie while he talks to him about the place they hope to have. The dramatic version has attempted to heighten the sense of conflict by playing upon the possibility that the others will interfere with what George must do; it has also objectified some of George's inner conflict by having Slim remain when the others have gone and offer by implication to do the deed for George. Throughout, the dramatic version has omitted some portions of action and added others in order to sharpen the focus of the conflicts on the stage. At the same time it has sacrificed the broader, in a sense more realistic, view of the situation found in the novel.

The possibilities of the novel form likewise enable Steinbeck to enter the minds of the characters in a way that is not possible in the play. The play must of necessity omit the scene at the end of the novel in which Lennie, hiding by the river before George comes, imagines first his Aunt Clara talking to him and then "a gigantic rabbit." In both hallucinations we see the working of Lennie's mind from a psychological point of view that can only be hinted at in the development of the action of the play.

The use of setting. Finally, the setting is the same for both play and novel; but in the play it inevitably remains a kind of backdrop, while in the novel it adds a symbolic dimension and sheds light on character and act. A "Production Note" in the dramatic version suggests that "no attempt should be made at realism" for the outdoor scene of Act I, scene 1, and that "the author's description of this scene should be regarded not as a technical requirement but simply in order to set the mood."[7] The stage directions themselves suggest a minimum of detail (and, of course, only details that are practicable on a stage):

A sandy bank of the Salinas River sheltered with willows—one giant sycamore up R. The stage is covered with dry leaves. The feeling is sheltered and quiet. Stage is lit by a setting sun. Curtain rises on empty stage. A sparrow is singing. There is a distant sound of ranch dogs barking aimlessly and one clear quail call. The quail call turns to a warning call and there is a beat of the flock's wings.

7. Steinbeck, *Of Mice and Men*, Dramatic version, p. 5.

Two figures are seen entering, L. or R., it makes no difference, in single file, with George, the short man, coming in ahead of Lennie. Both men are carrying blanket rolls. They approach the water. The small man throws down his blanket roll, the large man follows, then falls down and drinks from the river, snorting as he drinks.

GEORGE.   *(Irritably.)* Lennie, for God's sake, don't drink so much. *(Leans over and shakes Lennie.)* Lennie, you hear me! You gonna be sick like you was last night.[8]

Here, in contrast, are the opening paragraphs of the novel:

A few miles south of Soledad, the Salinas River drops in close to the hillside bank and runs deep and green. The water is warm too, for it has slipped twinkling over the yellow sands in the sunlight before reaching the narrow pool. On one side of the river the golden foothill slopes curve up to the strong and rocky Gabilan mountains, but on the valley side the water is lined with trees—willows fresh and green with every spring, carrying in their lower leaf junctures the debris of the winter's flooding; and sycamores with mottled, white, recumbent limbs and branches that arch over the pool. On the sandy bank under the trees the leaves lie deep and so crisp that a lizard makes a great skittering if he runs among them. Rabbits come out of the brush to sit on the sand in the evening, and the damp flats are covered with the night tracks of 'coons, and with the spread pads of dogs from the ranches, and with the split-wedge tracks of deer that come to drink in the dark.

There is a path through the willows and among the sycamores, a path beaten hard by boys coming down from the ranches to swim in the deep pool, and beaten hard by tramps who come wearily down from the highway in the evening to jungle-up near water. In front of the low horizontal limb of a giant sycamore there is an ash pile made by many fires; the limb is worn smooth by men who have sat on it.

Evening of a hot day started the little wind to moving among the leaves. The shade climbed up the hills toward the top. On the sand banks the rabbits sat as quietly as little gray, sculptured stones. And then from the direction of the state highway came the sound of footsteps on crisp sycamore leaves. The rabbits hurried noiselessly for cover. A stilted heron labored up into the

8. *Ibid.*, p. 7.

air and pounded down river. For a moment the place was lifeless, and then two men emerged from the path and came into the opening by the green pool.

They had walked in single file down the path, and even in the open one stayed behind the other. Both were dressed in denim trousers and in denim coats with brass buttons. Both wore black, shapeless hats and both carried tight blanket rolls slung over their shoulders. The first man was small and quick, dark of face, with restless eyes and sharp, strong features. Every part of him was defined: small, strong hands, slender arms, a thin and bony nose. Behind him walked his opposite, a huge man, shapeless of face, with large, pale eyes, with wide, sloping shoulders; and he walked heavily, dragging his feet a little, the way a bear drags his paws. His arms did not swing at his sides, but hung loosely.

The first man stopped short in the clearing, and the follower nearly ran over him. He took off his hat and wiped the sweatband with his forefinger and snapped the moisture off. His huge companion dropped his blankets and flung himself down and drank from the surface of the green pool; drank with long gulps, snorting into the water like a horse. The small man stepped nervously beside him.

"Lennie!" he said sharply. "Lennie, for God's sakes don't drink so much." Lennie continued to snort into the pool. The small man leaned over and shook him by the shoulder. "Lennie. You gonna be sick like you was last night."[9]

In the opening section of the novel the narrator has been able to give a good preliminary sketch of both characters before either speaks. There is the contrast between George's figure with "every part . . . defined," and Lennie's "shapeless . . . face" and heavy walk. There are the suggestions of Lennie's animal-like nature through the phrases "the way a bear drags his paws" and "snorting into the water like a horse" (the latter detail retained in the stage directions for the play, but with less emphasis, since an audience might not make the explicit comparison). Even more important, in the novel the scene has been described before the arrival of the men and the description reinforces our understanding of character, event, and theme, preparing us for things to come later in the book. It is a scene in which man and nature meet, with the well-worn path and the limb of the sycamore, "worn smooth by men who have sat on it," testifying to man's intrusion into the peaceful world of the river, the

9. Steinbeck, *Of Mice and Men,* Novel version, pp. 1–3.

lizards, the rabbits, the raccoons, and the deer. The state highway is only a short distance away, an ominous reminder of the nearness of civilization to this idyllic scene—at the end of the novel Slim leads George "up toward the highway" after the final tragedy. Thus, in the novel the initial setting prefigures the major conflicts between Lennie's simple animality and the complexities of society and between George and Lennie's dream of having a place of their own where they might live in harmony with nature and the constant intrusions of the world of human beings into that dream. These symbolic overtones of the scene are implied in the novel by the narrator, but in the play they can barely be hinted at in stage direction and staging. A sensitive reader should be able to detect and appreciate these differences.

Play and novel: major distinctions

Let us now codify some of the differences between novel and play in order to understand the two forms more fully and determine some implications for the teaching of each. The differences seem to center in three major distinctions:

"Now" vs. "then." Arthur Miller describes the first major distinction well when he says: "It's a difference between a past and a present tense, psychologically speaking. The drama is always *now*. A narrative is the past. In a play, something is being developed in front of you, rather than in retrospect."[10] Another way of putting this is to say that dramas are written primarily to be produced upon a stage, novels are written to be read: a play *shows,* a novel *tells.* From this fact stem some corollaries about the relationship between author and audience and the experience of the members of the viewing or reading audience.

The dramatist, largely because of the sense of immediacy inherent in his form, must keep himself in the shadows; he cannot afford to intervene between the audience and the events on the stage. (Apparent exceptions to this might be cited—the chorus in Greek drama, for example, or the Stage Manager in Thornton Wilder's *Our Town*— but in these cases the intervention is not directly by the author, since both chorus and Stage Manager become, in a sense, characters in the play.) The dramatist works in a form which calls for very tight control. He must remain outside the play, yet manage character and event in such a way that the audience react strongly to each step in the development of the action. On the simplest level, the audience must silently cheer the hero and boo the villain (and they sometimes even do this out loud). On a more complex level, the audience must share or

---

10. "An Interview with Arthur Miller," in Alan B. Howes, *Teaching Literature to Adolescents: Plays* (Glenview, Ill.: Scott, Foresman and Company, 1968), p. 106.

understand the feelings of characters at the precise moments when events are unfolding on the stage. The very nature of the form helps the dramatist to achieve this response in his audience: whether the stage be a platform, a screen, or a television tube—or even a stage in the mind as one reads—the attention of spectator or reader is bound to be focused constantly on the present and the events that are taking place before him.

The fact that the present tense, the *now* of the play, is alien to the novel can be seen in the awkwardness that is usually produced by any very lengthy excursion by the novelist into the historical present. This point is amusingly made in Robert Benchley's parody of the epistolary novel (though, of course, the epistolary novel need not employ the present tense). Benchley imagines the heroine of an epistolary novel describing events as they happen to her:

Monday night. Later.

DEAREST ANNA:—Now, indeed, it is evident, my best, my old friend, that I am face to face with the bitterest of fates. You will remember that in my last letter I spoke to you of a party of unprincipled knaves who were invading my apartment. And now do I find that they have, in furtherance of their inexcusable plans, set fire to that portion of the house which lies directly behind this, so that as I put my pen to paper the flames are creeping, like hungry creatures of some sort, through the partitions and into this very room, so that did I esteem my safety more than my correspondence with you, my precious companion, I should at once be making preparation for immediate departure. O my dear! To be thus seized, as I am at this very instant, by the unscrupulous leader of the band and carried, by brute force, down the stairway through the butler's pantry and into the servants' hall, writing as I go, resting my poor paper on the shoulder of my detested abductor, is truly, you will agree, my sweet Anna, a pitiable episode.

Adieu, my intimate friend.

Your obt. s'v't,
CL. HARLOWE.[11]

A number of things contribute to the humor of this passage and help to make it ridiculous, but none more than the use of the present tense. The novelist cannot usually afford to try to gain the immediacy of the dramatist. Just as the reader of drama must be aware of himself as a

11. Robert Benchley, "When Genius Remained Your Humble Servant," in *Benchley Beside Himself,* 12th ed. (New York: Harper & Row, Publishers, Inc., 1930), p. 79.

member of an audience watching the unfolding of a dramatic action, so the reader of a novel must be aware of some distance, of the fact that there is a teller of the tale he reads. He must realize that he sees the story through the eyes of a narrator who is reflecting on the past, rather than through his own eyes as he experiences the present on a stage before him.

The visual images of the drama presented on the stage in front of the playgoer will thus differ from the visual images produced in the mind of the novel reader. In the play, language joins with costume, action, gesture—all the accoutrements of stage production—to produce the effects, while in the novel the imagination of the reader must be stirred by words alone. Even if the play is read, the quality of the visual images will be somewhat different and will be determined in part by our conventional knowledge of what action on the stage looks like (and may, of course, be further defined through specific stage directions). The images called up by the novel, on the other hand, are scenes which are first imagined by the author and then reported and described to us from the point of view which the narrator chooses to adopt. We see a play through our own eyes as we watch a stage or imagine one in our minds; we see the action of a novel through the eyes of the man telling the tale as he chooses the words to convey the scene to us.

Extended vs. restricted time and space. If the first major distinction between the play and the novel is the difference between a past and a present tense, the second is the accompanying limitation of time and space in the drama. The physical dimensions of the stage place limitations upon the action of the play, and the conventional amount of time for an average production places further restrictions upon the scope of what can be presented. One can understand these limitations more clearly by comparing both stage play and novel with the motion picture, which is an interesting hybrid—the offspring of the other two forms, in a sense. More purely visual than the drama, the motion picture relies less upon linguistic stimuli. The camera, with its flexibility of movement, can convey things to us which a stage playwright could manage only through dialogue. Thus the action of a motion picture has more of the wider ranging possibilities of the novel, though the action will be presented visually rather than through a narrator.

One can see the difference between action presented in a motion picture and action described in a novel—though both provide greater scope than the stage—by considering what happens when the motion picture action is reduced to words. Here, from the novelization of the motion picture, is the description of King Kong's first appearance (the native tribe are gathered at night on top of a gigantic wall just outside their village; on the other side of the wall is a stone altar with a platform a dozen feet above the ground; the natives have just bound Ann between the two pillars of the altar, a sacrifice to Kong, and have retreated to the top of the wall to watch Kong's approach):

> From the shadowed base of the precipice came a deep, unreal roar which met the roll of the drum and threw it back against the wall.
> "Kong!" The watching, torch-illumined mob on the rampart burst into a great cry. "Kong! Kong! Kong!"
>
> Before her, she became conscious of the crowded wall. Behind her she was aware of a closer, deeper shout, and of a Shadow. She turned her head. Then, while her eyes widened, the Shadow split the black cloak of the precipice and became solidly real. Blinking up at the packed wall, its vast mouth roared defiance, its black, furred hands drummed a black, furred breast in challenge. In the full glare of the torches it hesitated, stopped and as though reading the meaning of the thousand hands which gestured from the rampart, turned and looked down at the altar, and at Ann.
> It did not look *up* at Ann upon her pedestal. It looked *down*. Moving closer it stared down between the two pillars. . . .
> Immediately [King Kong] found that he could not pick Ann up, and shortly he found the reason. The ropes, however, offered no difficulty. . . . In an intensity of preoccupation he began to rumble to himself as he turned the figure over, this way and that, much in the manner that a half-adult human being might turn and inspect a limp unconscious bird. . . .
> With a last, intent look at the white countenance beneath his hand, he shifted Ann's form to the crook of one arm and started slowly back into the shadow of the precipice.[12]

Anyone who has seen the motion picture will miss in this prose version the awesome images that were captured on film. The novelizer attempts to compensate for this lack by insisting that Kong looked *down* not *up*, and by the metaphor of the human being holding the unconscious bird; but these cannot convey the power that the movie scene did, although the metaphor begins to create a powerful effect of its own, an effect possible for the novelist but not the film-maker.

The writer who starts with a tale to tell in words rather than on

---

12. Edgar Wallace and Merian C. Cooper, *King Kong*, novelization by Delos W. Lovelace (New York: Bantam Books, Inc., 1965), Ch. 9, pp. 69–71.

film works rather differently, for he cannot rely directly on visual images apart from the words that he uses to create them, apart from description, connotation, metaphor, and symbol. And though a picture may not be worth a thousand words—the two cannot really be compared—a picture creates one kind of effect in the viewer; words—ten or a thousand—create another kind of effect. In creating his verbal picture the writer must find a way to reach the reader's imagination: he will select details that suggest; he will emphasize parts of the scene, leaving other parts shadowy; he will rely on metaphor and implication. Compare the passage above describing the appearance of King Kong, which has its origin in a motion picture sequence, with this description of Grendel in *Beowulf*, which has its origin in a storyteller's imagination:

> Then Grendel, bearer of God's anger, came from the moor, keeping in the shadows of the misty cliffs. The evil demon thought to trap some of the men in the great hall. He came under the dark skies toward the place where he knew he would find the men's wine-hall, gleaming with gold. This was not the first time he had come to attack Hrothgar's house, but never in all the days of his life did he meet with a bitterer fate or braver warriors. The joyless ravager made his way to the hall. The door, fastened with metal bands tempered in fire, at once gave way to his hands. Enraged and bent on evil, the fiend swung open the door and stepped, quick and angry, onto the shining floor. A horrible light gleamed like fire from his eyes.[13]

The *Beowulf* poet does not give any specific statement about Grendel's size in this passage describing the monster's first appearance, although later in the poem we gather something of Grendel's size from the fact that four men were required to carry his severed head. The writer of the novelized version of *King Kong*, attempting to re-create some of the effects captured on film, takes care to give us the dimensions of the stone altar and to say that Kong looked *down* not *up* at the platform. In *Beowulf*, the "misty cliffs," the "wine-hall, gleaming with gold," the "shining floor" are all described evocatively rather than specifically. The metaphor of fire is used to describe the light from Grendel's eyes (just as the writer of the novelization of *King Kong* moves in the direction of the typical novelist's technique with the metaphor of the "limp unconscious bird," a metaphor which cannot be shown directly on the screen).

13. Translated by Alan B. Howes and Lidie M. Howes from Fr[iedrich] Klaeber, ed., *Beowulf*, 3rd ed. (Lexington, Mass.: D. C. Heath and Company, 1936), ll. 710–727.

More important, the *Beowulf* poet can characterize Grendel's state of mind: he is "bearer of God's anger," a "joyless ravager" who is "enraged and bent on evil." King Kong's motives and mental state—less important in the film, where the action itself is the focus of attention—must be stated somewhat awkwardly: "In the full glare of the torches it hesitated, stopped and as though reading the meaning of the thousand hands which gestured from the rampart, turned and looked down at the altar, and at Ann." Finally, the narrator in *Beowulf* is present in a way that is made possible only by the narrative genre. He comments that "never in all the days of his life did [Grendel] meet with a bitterer fate or braver warriors." The knowledge of both past and future is part of the narrative writer's possible point of view (whether he discloses this knowledge or not), while the film-maker (unless he uses flashbacks—and their appropriateness is usually limited to a major or extended sequence of action—or has a narrator speaking while we look at action in the present on the screen) is bound to the knowledge of the present that the camera can convey. The motion picture relies mainly on visual images and scenes of present action to tell its story; the novel or the long narrative tells its story through a narrator, who may, of course, reveal more or less of himself and his own attitude, but who is always there, relaying the action to us, filtering it first through a distinctive point of view. Even though the camera's selectivity represents a point of view, the selectivity must in general be limited to the present and the scene before us; the writer of narrative is freer to bring past and present together and is able to black out parts of any scene more completely than the film-maker does in conventional film techniques. The writer of narrative also has the advantages of all the resources of language: metaphor, symbol, connotation. These must be used by the dramatist within the context of dialogue spoken by the characters on stage or screen. Though film differs from stage play, both belong to a larger genre in which the *now,* the present tense, is both advantage and limitation and is contrasted with the *then* of the novel.

Concentrated vs. panoramic form. The third major difference between drama and narrative results from the differences between present and past tense and between limited and relatively unlimited use of time and space. The dramatist, bound to the present and its limits of time and space, must develop his story in concentrated form, since the time he has available for confrontation with his audience is limited and the space of the stage is rigidly defined. (Even though the stage may be made to represent a number of settings in fairly quick sequence, the spatial limits of any one setting are fixed.) In addition to this physical limitation, there is likewise a psychological limitation on

the range of time and space that an audience can absorb through their
senses as they watch a play. If they are to be brought to a sense of the
importance of the past, it must be through demonstration of that
importance in the present. The novelist, on the other hand, may count
upon a leisurely or extended reading of his story, and hence may tell it
in a more leisurely or extended way. He may ask his audience by
implication (or even occasionally by direct request) to compare one
part of his tale with another, and may picture a much wider and more
diffuse set of circumstances surrounding the events of his tale. Even in
the two very similar versions of *Of Mice and Men* considered above,
Act II, scene 2 of the play concentrates on the central conflict of the
action involving George and Lennie, while the corresponding Chapter
Four of the novel focuses for the moment on Crooks. In the novel, the
different parts of the story may be told from multiple perspectives;
while the form of the drama is concentrated, the form of the novel is
more often panoramic.

Of course, neither dramatist nor novelist can afford to ignore the
whole chain of cause and effect that leads to significant human action.
It is simply that the dramatist, most characteristically, cannot spend
much time in exploring causes apart from their immediately obvious
effects upon the stage. He is likely to assume a background of causes
for the immediate action rather than develop one in detail, for he
must build quickly toward complication and climax. In a play like
Oedipus Rex, for example, Sophocles chooses to begin with the plague
in the city rather than with the striking down of Laius some fifteen
years before or with the prediction of the Oracle and the abandonment
of Oedipus by Laius and Jocasta many years before that. In *Macbeth,*
Duncan is killed early in Act II and the rest of the play explores the
consequences of Macbeth's deed and the degeneration of his character—though, obviously, many events before the opening of the play
contributed to Macbeth's decision to murder Duncan. Even in a play
like *Hamlet,* where the apparent focus is upon Hamlet's process of
decision (and hence upon the causes that lead to the final tragic
results), Shakespeare does not go back, as a novelist might have, to
the murder of Hamlet's father and the adulterous connection between
Gertrude and Claudius, except by report of the Ghost, and we see no
scenes of Hamlet's childhood and upbringing, though these must
have played a part in shaping the character we see on the stage. *Death
of a Salesman* might serve as a final example of variation within this
overall pattern of similarity: Willy Loman's past is explored in some
detail through psychological flashbacks, but only as an understanding
of it contributes to an understanding of the present and of the issues
facing the man we see before us on the stage.

The novelist, in contrast, is more apt to deal at length with the chain of causes that leads to an important choice or series of choices, which in turn produce significant effects, and to specify more of the surrounding circumstances for these choices. We see much more of Raskolnikov in *Crime and Punishment* than of Macbeth before the time that each commits murder. We follow Tom Jones and David Copperfield from their births before seeing them finally united with their beloveds; in the plays *The Tempest* and *The Taming of the Shrew,* in contrast, the love story of Ferdinand and Miranda occupies only hours, while Petruchio tames his Kate in a matter of days. Even an apparent exception like Hemingway's novel *For Whom the Bell Tolls,* which covers an action of only three days, contains scenes outside the present action—Pilar's account of the massacre of the Fascists at the beginning of the war, for example—which would be difficult to present on the stage and still retain the dramatist's concern with the *now* (though the motion picture version managed the massacre scene through a flashback as Pilar recounted the episode).

The dramatist will be criticized if there is too much exposition and hence a delay in the action. The novelist, not bound to the *now,* but free to lead us to reflect upon the past, is likely to explore a series of causes and to give us a richer background for understanding specific actions rather than concentrating on a single crisis in the action.

Accordingly, we frequently find a pattern of oscillation in the action of a novel which would be inappropriate or unmanageable for a play, where the action must move forward rapidly from causes to final effects. In the novel, the tale is built around recurring motifs in the action, as events which are similar to previous events are played out in different settings or circumstances. Rather than moving directly to climax and resolution, the novelist frequently circles around a central situation, increasing our knowledge of characters as we see them reacting (perhaps in slightly different ways) to similar situations. In James Fenimore Cooper, for example, the recurring pattern of action is capture-escape-pursuit, while in Fielding's *Tom Jones* the pattern is impulse-action-consequence as we trace Tom's indiscretions and his ups and downs in his quest for Sophia. Even novels as different as *Pamela* and *Invisible Man* share the pattern of hope-betrayal-despair as Richardson chronicles Pamela's struggle with Mr. B. or as Ellison traces his hero's search for identity in a society which promises at one moment and denies at the next. The repetition of such patterns in the novel produces a series of rising actions, each with its own climax and resolution; the dramatist, though he builds his play on a series of minor climaxes, focuses them all toward a major climax followed by a final resolution. The novelist, though he must provide a resolution for the entire action of his novel, is usually freer in the working out of that resolution and less apt to center our attention on a single climax.

Summary

A number of implications for the teaching of drama and the novel that arise from the similarities and differences between the forms have already been touched upon. These implications and others will now be made more explicit, by way both of summary and of amplification:

1. Both drama and novel are relatively long forms in which it is often difficult to get students to perceive the relationship between whole and parts. Given the attention and interest spans of most adolescents, it is important in the teaching of both forms not to let a consideration of the details, the parts, obscure students' understanding of the whole. Knowledge of *all* the details of the plot, of the identities of *all* the minor characters, should willingly be sacrificed in the interest of an understanding of the main sweep of the action, the thematic implications of major characters. The longer the work, the greater the possibility of bogging down in meaningless details that never become related to the whole; and if a blow-by-blow presentation of a play is usually ill-advised, such an approach to most novels is disastrous.

2. While an understanding of the whole work should take precedence over a detailed consideration of insignificant parts, at the same time significant details must be understood if students are to understand the whole. Here the selection of details for emphasis by the teacher is crucial. In drama, those details should be emphasized which contribute to an understanding of staging: this means calling attention to stage directions and inventing stage directions suggested by clues in the dialogue. In the novel, those details should be emphasized which contribute to an understanding of point of view: this means calling attention to clues in the language itself which betray the attitude of the narrator. In both forms details which give an insight into characters should be stressed: this means paying attention to both actions and words which reveal motive, conflict, and ultimately theme.

3. In both drama and the novel the major source of student attention and interest lies in characters and what they do, rather than in a more technical and abstract consideration of the plot. Adolescents enjoy watching characters in action, speculating on the reasons for the

way they act, identifying with or rejecting them, and agreeing or disagreeing with the reasons behind their actions. They do not enjoy—nor profit from—mere memorization of the order of a sequence of events, unless that sequence takes on some reality through an understanding of the human motivations behind it. Students will not be satisfied with knowing merely the plot, the *what*—they will want to discuss the motivations of characters, the *why*. And in order to understand both *what* and *why*, they must be able to visualize what the characters do on the stage and, for the novel, what the point of view of the narrator is.

4. In drama, the *now*—the perspective of the present tense, of a series of events unfolding before the eyes of the spectator—means that the teacher should try to get students to re-create the action in all the richness of a stage production. The student should also be led to think of himself as a member of an audience and helped and encouraged to respond as an audience does. To supplement the usually scanty stage directions, the student should be directed to look in the text of the play for linguistic clues to what is happening on the stage—hints as to gesture, facial expression, movement, stage business, and (not least) lighting, costuming, and scenery. The drama *shows,* and he must be aware of what would be shown in a stage production. At the same time he should be led to respond to each part of the play as it unfolds before him, even if only in the theatre of the mind.

5. In the novel, the *then*—the fact that the novelist reflects upon the past (explicitly or implicitly) as he recounts it—means that students can fully understand what is told only as they recognize the teller of the tale and adjust their perspective as readers to that of the narrator. An understanding of point of view is crucial, whether it be first or third person, omnipotent author or limited author, novelist or persona. Clues to point of view in the novel, like clues to the action on a stage, come through words, and hence a close look at the language in key passages is essential in both.

6. Adolescents will enjoy the fast pace of the action of a play, but they may overlook important parts of it because the action is so concentrated. In the novel, the fact that motifs in the action are often repeated in an apparent pattern of oscillation means that students have more time to acquaint themselves with characters and hence may be able to understand them more fully; but they may also feel that the novel is static and they may miss minor but significant variations in

the repetition of motif. To counter these difficulties, the teacher should stress motives for action in both cases, so that the rapid pace of the drama will not seem bewildering and the more leisurely developed action of the novel can be seen as leading somewhere.

7. Finally, the novel, as a form, seems to both demand and invite a somewhat more flexible teaching approach than the drama. Because of its length, the novel is more apt to be assigned for out-of-class reading; because of the looser, more panoramic nature of its form, it is more appropriate for such assignments. This means that teachers will probably want to work out ways for teaching the novel through individualized reading programs (more of this later). Also, a given novel is more apt to be appropriate for reading in different ways at different levels than is a given play. Novels like *Huckleberry Finn* or *A Separate Peace,* for example, can be read with both pleasure and profit by students all the way from junior high to graduate school. It is difficult to think of plays which are equally appropriate for such widely differing levels. But whatever level and approach, the teacher should try to teach both drama and novel for the unique satisfactions inherent in each generic form.

PART TWO

The Nature of Narrative

Narrative plays an earlier, more continuous, and more important part in most people's lives than any other kind of literature. Children begin with fairy tales and move on to the more sophisticated children's stories they read both in and out of school. *Peter Rabbit* and Dr. Seuss are supplanted by *Stuart Little, Charlotte's Web,* and *The Wind in the Willows.* Younger adolescents read junior books—Tarzan and Nancy Drew and Sue Barton—and, perhaps a little later, *The Light in the Forest, The Catcher in the Rye,* and *A Separate Peace.* Adults read novels—best sellers or classics—detective stories, and stories in magazines. Adults likewise repeat stories to each other when they meet on the street corner or at a party; they rarely recite poetry or quote from plays.

Knowing that adolescents are likely to feel most at home with narrative (provided, at least, it is in prose), some teachers may feel that all they need do is set novels before their students and start them reading; others, fearing that "mere" enjoyment of fiction is somehow not a solid enough goal, belabor their students with a mass of historical, biographical, and critical background, which becomes an end in itself. Wise teachers avoid both these extremes: adolescent readers need some guidance in order to read with greater understanding and enjoyment, and historical or biographical background may contribute to the understanding and enjoyment of individual books, but it must be presented as a means to those ends. A knowledge of critical theory can likewise increase students' pleasure in what they read if it, too, is presented as a means of entry into books. Leading students to greater enjoyment of what they read is a perfectly respectable goal, and background materials of all sorts may be useful in achieving that goal.

With these principles in mind, let us look briefly at a few statements by novelists and critics, chosen to suggest the wide disagreements and multiplicity of issues that have characterized the history of criticism of the novel. We will indicate some of the ways in which an awareness of these issues might be helpful to the teacher and then discuss some of the elements that are basic in all kinds of narrative. Finally, we shall consider the reading process itself, in order to find ways that the teacher can help students enjoy and profit from the reading of fiction. The teacher's primary purpose in assessing this material should be to draw upon critical theory in helping students become more appreciative readers of fiction.

Problems in definition

Although narrative is one of the oldest kinds of literature, the novel is not only the latest of the major literary genres to arrive on the scene, but also the genre that has been least amenable to precise definition and analysis by literary critics. Early in its history, Henry Fielding tried to connect the novel with earlier narrative traditions by calling his own *Joseph Andrews* (1742) "a comic epic poem in prose."[1] Though today this may seem an odd way to go about defining the novel, Fielding was writing for an audience that was well-grounded in classical critical traditions and familiar with the *Iliad,* the *Odyssey,* the *Aeneid,* and the whole body of classical literature. He thought of his own book as a "kind of writing . . . not . . . hitherto attempted in our language," but he felt that it was at the same time a logical extension of earlier traditions. Its affinity with the epic lay in its exact "copying of nature," and this distinguished it both from the prose romance (or "serious romance") and from burlesque. In contrast to the serious romance, Fielding's book is "light and ridiculous" rather than "grave and solemn" in its tone; its characters are "of inferior rank" rather than noble; it aims at "the ludicrous instead of the sublime." In summary, it shares with the prose romance only the fact of being written in prose. It likewise differs from burlesque, he says, since burlesque aims at exaggeration and caricature rather than at an exact copying of nature. The issue here is whether realism—the exact copying of nature or fidelity to everyday life—is central to the novel. Fielding's assertion that it is has been borne out by subsequent

---

1. This and other quotations from the Author's Preface, *The Adventures of Joseph Andrews and His Friend Mr. Abraham Adams,* ed. by George Saintsbury (London: J. M. Dent and Company, 1893).

history, for the novel has retained this affinity for realism in spite of some exceptions. Fielding also classifies his kind of writing as comic, and this strain has likewise persisted in the novel, even though the possibilities for tragedy have been more fully explored in the novel than Fielding might have thought possible.

In the century following Fielding, fidelity to everyday life had become so much a part of the tradition of the novel that Nathaniel Hawthorne felt the need to defend his choice of the romance, his own manner of storytelling. Writing in 1851, he says: "When a writer calls his work a Romance, it need hardly be observed that he wishes to claim a certain latitude, both as to its fashion and material, which he would not have felt himself entitled to assume, had he professed to be writing a Novel." The novel, he continues, "is presumed to aim at a very minute fidelity, not merely to the possible, but to the probable and ordinary course of man's experience," while the romance presents "the truth of the human heart . . . under circumstances, to a great extent, of the writer's own choosing or creation."[2] Perhaps the most important critical issue that Hawthorne raises is that of the relationship between the writer and his readers. Hawthorne feels that the writer has a duty to stick within the commonly accepted limitations of the particular genre or subgenre in which he writes. Hawthorne chose the romance as the form most congenial for expressing his particular view of "the truth of the human heart," but he recognized that his readers, accustomed to a different sort of technique in the novel, would need to be warned what to expect.

Nearly a century later, when novels had become the daily fare of a mass audience, Wyndham Lewis makes the key distinction between the flood of fiction which is "just a slovenly blah . . . a sort of folk-prose of the Middle-Classes of Western Democracy" and those works of fiction which are truly "literature."[3] Lewis raises (perhaps a bit snobbishly) the important issue of quality. He regrets that we have no terminology to make distinctions in quality, for he believes that since "fiction" has come to be regarded as a serious art, critical standards have fallen. He apparently thinks of "fiction" as a separate and inferior class from "literature," though some works of fiction would qualify as literature. He seems to be more interested in separating good novels from bad novels than in separating the novel from other kinds of literature.

More recently, Northrop Frye has tried to make sense of the

2. Nathaniel Hawthorne, Author's Preface, January 27, 1851, *The House of Seven Gables* (Boston: Houghton, Mifflin and Company, 1879).
3. Wyndham Lewis, "The Taxi-Cab Driver Test for 'Fiction,'" *Men Without Art* (London: Cassell and Company, Ltd., 1934), p. 296.

tangled skeins in the history of criticism of the novel by calling
attention to "the four forms of fiction"—novel, romance, confession,
and anatomy.[4] We need to recognize, he says, "a distinction . . . between fiction as a genus and the novel as a species of that genus"; and
further, we should note the possibilities for various combinations of
the four diverse forms of fiction in books we call "novels." "The
romancer," Frye says, "does not attempt to create 'real people' so
much as stylized figures which expand into psychological archetypes,"
and the romance "often radiates a glow of subjective intensity that the
novel lacks, and . . . a suggestion of allegory is constantly creeping in
around its fringes." *Wuthering Heights, The House of the Seven
Gables,* and *Pilgrim's Progress* are among the examples of romance
that Frye cites. The confession has its roots in autobiography, and
"nearly always some theoretical and intellectual interest in religion,
politics, or art plays a leading role" in it. Examples that Frye gives
include St. Augustine's *Confessions,* Rousseau's *Confessions,* and
Moll Flanders. The anatomy (also called the Menippean satire) "deals
less with people as such than with mental attitudes"; in its "most
concentrated" form it "presents us with a vision of the world in terms
of a single intellectual pattern." Among the examples Frye cites are
Gulliver's Travels, Candide, Brave New World, Alice in Wonderland,
and Burton's *Anatomy of Melancholy.* In contrast to the other three,
the novel as a "pure" form attempts "to create 'real people,'" and "to
dissolve all theory into personal relationships"; "its chief interest is in
human character as it manifests itself in society." But the novel is
seldom found in its "pure" state and frequently—as some of the
examples above suggest—is found in combination with one or more of
the other three forms of prose fiction. Thus, Frye says, Joyce's *Portrait
of the Artist as a Young Man* combines novel and confession, *Moby
Dick* combines romance and anatomy (and is not, in Frye's terms, a
novel), and *Don Quixote* blends elements of novel, anatomy, and
romance.

It should be clear even from this brief and selective discussion that
the critics and novelists who have attempted to define the novel ever
since its inception have failed to agree on any set of criteria for
distinguishing the novel from other genres, though the connection
with everyday life and real people is a thread running through many of
the critical statements. These and other critics have raised issues of
quality, of the relationship of the writer to the reader, and of the kind
of technique and view of the world appropriate to the novel. They

---

4. This and other quotations from Northrop Frye, "Specific Continuous Forms (Prose Fiction), "
The Anatomy of Criticism: Four Essays (Princeton, N.J.: Princeton University Press, 1957), pp.
303–312.

have not agreed on bases for definition or analysis, but, rather, have found alternative critical perspectives that range from form to content, from quality to technique. This uncertainty still plagues critics, and the teacher may well be bewildered by such lack of agreement as he attempts to make the reading of novels representing a particular literary genre a unique experience for his students.

But there is an important implication for the teacher to be found in the very disagreements of the critics. These disagreements suggest that it is unwise to give students too rigid or precise a definition for the novel, and further (most strongly suggested in Frye but also implicit in Fielding and Hawthorne) that each work of fiction must be judged on its own terms. *The House of the Seven Gables* or *Wuthering Heights* should not be read and judged in the same way as, say, *David Copperfield* or *Babbitt:* the former pair make no pretense to complete "realism"; the latter pair do. *Gulliver's Travels* should not be faulted because Gulliver is an inconsistent character, sometimes the vehicle for expressing Swift's satire, sometimes the object of it; Swift is not writing a novel, but a different kind of fiction in which idea takes precedence over character. Utopian and science fiction stories demand a special kind of reading; students should be led to look for different things in *Erewhon* or *1984* or *Fahrenheit 451* than they do in *Great Expectations* or *The Grapes of Wrath* or *The Scarlet Letter.* Both ideas and characters play a part in each of these, but the relationship between idea and character in each is different. Though it is not the teacher's function to make aesthetic theorists out of his adolescent readers (and hence generic definitions are not important for their own sake), it is important for the teacher to arrive at the kind of theoretical or generic understanding of individual works of fiction that can be translated into classroom approaches which will help his students respond to the books they read. It is not important for students to come away from a course with a knowledge of the history of the novel, but it is important for them to respond appropriately to each work that they read. And appropriate response comes from taking each book on its own terms.

Narrative is a very loose term covering everything from the *Odyssey* to Joyce's *Ulysses,* from "Edward" or "Lord Randal" to *Wuthering Heights,* from *Hiroshima* to *Gulliver's Travels* to *Lord of the Flies.* It is important for students to see the parallels between novels and other kinds of narrative if they are to read each kind of book with maximum understanding. Northrop Frye points out that the novel is a species of the genus fiction. One might add that even historical narratives like *Hiroshima* share important qualities with works of fiction, and that narrative is commonly found in certain kinds of poetry as well as in prose. These diverse kinds of narrative can be best taught if each is related to some general characteristics applicable to all narrative. We shall determine some of these general characteristics, noting at the same time some of the implications which follow for teaching specific kinds of narrative.

Elements common to all narrative

The two elements common to all narrative are a narrator and a stream of events in the past—recollected or imagined. (Even if the events are in the future, historically speaking, as they often are in science fiction, they are nearly always related in the past tense.) The narrator may appear to know everything about the story he is telling, or very little; he may be an omniscient author, a persona assumed by the author, or a character—major or minor—in the story itself. In any event, the author will have decided upon a point of view for his narrator. Decisions about point of view involve two choices: (1) What portion of the total stream of events is the narrator to be allowed to see, understand, and recount? (2) What attitude toward the story and toward the reader is the narrator to adopt? These decisions will, in turn, determine what we are told and how it is arranged, and what our attitude (though it may not coincide with that of the narrator) will be.

Though we may think of "point of view" as a critical term for a sophisticated technique only to be found in novels like those of Henry James, in actuality, every successful narrator must adopt a point of view, no matter what sort of story he is telling. Notice the way the narrator of this children's story establishes a point of view:

> It was a quiet summer afternoon, and Harvey Muskrat was building a raft in the backyard. He was hammering hard when his big sister Mildred stuck her head out of the window.
> "Harvey, you stop that hammering!" said Mildred.
> "I can't," said Harvey. "I'm building a raft."
> "Build it someplace else," said Mildred. "I'm writing a poem."
> "I can't," said Harvey. "This is where the hammer and nails and all my planks and logs are. Why don't you go someplace else to write your poem?"
> "It's my house as much as it is yours," said Mildred.
> "And it's my backyard as much as it is yours," said Harvey.
> "You are being selfish and inconsiderate," said Mildred, "and I'm telling."
> "Go ahead and tell," said Harvey, and he went on hammering until his mother came out on the back porch.
> "Harvey," said Mother, "that is a terrible racket to make so

close to the house. You really ought to do your hammering somewhere else."

"So, ha ha ha," said Mildred, and she stuck out her tongue at Harvey.

Harvey stuck out his tongue back at Mildred. Then he piled his tools on his planks and logs and swam with them to the other side of the pond to finish his hammering. When the raft was finished, Harvey poled it back across the pond and went fishing on the raft where Mildred could see him from her window.

When Mildred saw Harvey, she called, "Can I have a ride on the raft?"

"No," said Harvey, "because this is not the house and it is not the backyard and no part of it is yours. It is my raft and nobody else's. So, ha ha ha."

"That is just what I would expect from a selfish, inconsiderate, stupid, no-good little brother like you," said Mildred.

"That is because you are a loudmouth, bossy, mean and rotten big sister," said Harvey as Mother came out on the back porch again.

"You will both have to stop that right now," said Mother, "and your father is going to hear about it when he comes home."

When Father came rowing home in his boat and opened the front door he heard about it. "Mildred," said Father, "it is true that Harvey is selfish and inconsiderate, but he is not stupid and no-good, and you are not allowed to call him that."

"What about what he called me?" said Mildred.

"Mildred is loudmouthed and bossy," said Father to Harvey, "but she is not mean and rotten, and after supper both of you will have sentences to write."

So after supper Harvey had to write *I will not call Mildred mean and rotten* five hundred times. Mildred had to write *I will not call Harvey stupid and no-good* five hundred times.

"Well," said Mildred to Harvey when they had finished their sentences and were standing in the hallway outside their rooms, "you see how much trouble we got into, and that is what happens with selfish, inconsiderate, stupid, no-good little brothers."

"Only when they have loudmouth, bossy, mean and rotten big sisters," said Harvey.

Both of them spoke very quietly so that Mother and Father would not hear them. . . .

Then Mildred and Harvey stuck their tongues out at each other, slammed the doors of their rooms quietly, and went to bed.[5]

5. Russell Hoban, *Harvey's Hideout* (New York: Parents' Magazine Press, 1969), pp. 5–16.

Though this story may almost appear to tell itself, there is a narrator in the background, selecting details and using language very carefully to establish a point of view. The point of view is objective, partly because the narrator is not a character in the story—he is not more sympathetic to one child than to the other. He is amused at their squabble but he does not moralize about it. He has selected details that help to convey that amusement—the bits of dialogue he quotes, the fact that the children speak quietly as they continue their argument so that the parents can't hear them—and he has used language carefully to heighten the humor: they "slammed the doors of their rooms quietly." Nor is the point of view merely established for the benefit of any adult readers: children respond to the humor. A reader is anxious to hear more because he likes the way the story is being told as well as the story itself.

Point of view: selection and arrangement

Any story is potentially full of numerous details, many of them peripheral to the main action; and these details must be winnowed and ordered in meaningful sequence through a point of view if we are to give our allegiance and interest to a narrator. To understand the importance of selection and arrangement—though we are often unaware of their importance as we read—we might try to imagine what a story would be like without them. Actually, Mark Twain has done this job for us: here is his account of a storyteller who simply "could *not* forget anything":

> Such a memory as that is a great misfortune. To it, all occurrences are of the same size. Its possessor cannot distinguish an interesting circumstance from an uninteresting one. As a talker, he is bound to clog his narrative with tiresome details and make himself an insufferable bore. Moreover, he cannot stick to his subject. He picks up every little grain of memory he discerns in his way, and so is led aside. Mr. Brown would start out with the honest intention of telling you a vastly funny anecdote about a dog. He would be "so full of laugh" that he could hardly begin; then his memory would start with the dog's breed and personal appearance; drift into a history of his owner; of his owner's family, with descriptions of weddings and burials that had occurred in it, together with recitals of congratulatory verses and obituary poetry provoked by the same; then this memory would recollect that one of these events occurred during the celebrated "hard winter" of such and such a year, and a minute description

of that winter would follow, along with the names of people who were frozen to death, and statistics showing the high figures which pork and hay went up to. Pork and hay would suggest corn and fodder; corn and fodder would suggest cows and horses; cows and horses would suggest the circus and certain celebrated bare-back riders; the transition from the circus to the menagerie was easy and natural; from the elephant to equatorial Africa was but a step; then of course the heathen savages would suggest religion; and at the end of three or four hours' tedious jaw, the watch would change, and Brown would go out of the pilot-house muttering extracts from sermons he had heard years before about the efficacy of prayer as a means of grace. And the original first mention would be all you had learned about that dog, after all this waiting and hungering.[6]

Mr. Brown was "an insufferable bore" because he had no control over the story he was telling. Control comes through the selection and arrangement of materials and determines not only how we will respond to a story, but indeed whether we will be interested enough in it to respond at all. Twain's control, in contrast to Brown's, is very tight. Though Brown leaps from subject to subject by what seems a set of chance associations, Twain has built up the series carefully. The rhythm quickens toward the end with the more rapid transitions from subject to subject and fewer details about each. And the humorous effect is heightened by Twain's ironic attitude: words like "easy and natural," "but a step," and "of course" are not to be taken at their face value; they suggest, rather, that Twain is laughing at Mr. Brown. We are interested in Twain's story; we would not have been interested in Brown's. Twain's story differs from Brown's in having a carefully established point of view.

Point of view: technical and thematic

There are two aspects to point of view—for convenience we may call them the *technical* and the *thematic*. The technical point of view is concerned first of all with what position in time the narrator will assume in telling his story. Will it be told chronologically or will the chronology be rearranged? In the passage quoted above, Twain, as narrator, moves chronologically; Mr. Brown, as narrator, does not. (Twain, of course, must have Brown wander away from chronology or the point of Twain's anecdote would be lost.) The technical point of

6. Samuel L. Clemens, *Life on the Mississippi* (Boston: James R. Osgood and Company, 1883), Ch. XIII, p. 158.

view is also concerned with space. Will the narrator move about freely from place to place (as an omniscient author often does) or will he be restricted in movement (as a character who is narrator usually must be)? Twain's focus necessarily remains on the scene in the pilot-house, while Mr. Brown, again of necessity for Twain's purpose, roams from the dog's family to the circus to the wilds of Africa. No particular technical point of view automatically assures success; it must be adapted to the narrator and his story.

Thematic point of view is usually somewhat more complicated. It is concerned with the narrator's attitude toward his story and its characters and also with his relationship with the reader. (The two, of course, are closely related, for the narrator usually tries, implicitly or explicitly, to get the reader to share his attitude toward characters and events.) Twain, as narrator, conveys an amused contempt for Mr. Brown, and he establishes a familiarity with the reader: he assumes both you and he understand how ridiculous Brown's way of telling a story is. He does this partly through initial comments about what a "great misfortune" Brown's memory is, partly through his choice of details, partly through the linguistic clues which show his ironic view of Brown. Mr. Brown, as narrator, does not establish a thematic point of view: he does not manage to make his story have a point around which to arrange the details nor to establish rapport with his audience; and the only feeling his hearers have is boredom and frustration.

There are many kinds of literary narrators, just as there are many kinds of storytellers in real life, and our interest in a story is determined by our interest in the teller more often than we realize. Likewise, difficulties in understanding may arise from a failure to grasp what a narrator is doing. No story really tells itself, however shadowy or objective the narrator may be, and if students are to respond fully to a story, they must be led to an understanding of who the narrator is and how he has chosen to tell his story. Let us examine a few of the most important distinctions about narrators that students might make in reference to point of view.

Omniscient vs. limited. Probably the most common and obvious distinction about narrators' points of view is between the *omniscient* and the *limited.* If the author chooses to tell the story himself with an omniscient point of view, he will be able to include in his story more than any single character could know, even though he may also decide on some self-imposed limitations to his omniscience. The opening of John Steinbeck's *The Pearl* is a good example of an author-narrator with an omniscient point of view:

Kino awakened in the near dark. The stars still shone and the day had drawn only a pale wash of light in the lower sky to the east. The roosters had been crowing for some time, and the early pigs were already beginning their ceaseless turning of twigs and bits of wood to see whether anything to eat had been overlooked. Outside the brush house in the tuna clump, a covey of little birds chittered and flurried with their wings.[7]

The narrator here tells what is going on both outside and inside the brush house and likewise both what is happening and what has been happening—the "roosters had been crowing for some time." He feels free to range in time and space in a manner that would be virtually impossible if the narrator were a character in the story. Kino, for example, as narrator would have to limit his account to what he could see or hear at any given moment from any given spot. He could not have heard the beginning of the roosters' crowing, since he was asleep, nor could he see the scene inside the house and that outside at the same moment.

Thus, if an author elects to have a character in his story (either major or minor) be narrator, he has automatically chosen a more limited point of view than that of the omniscient narrator, whether the story is to be told in the first or the third person. Sometimes, as in Somerset Maugham's *The Razor's Edge,* the character-narrator is merely a thinly disguised alternative to the omniscient author. Here is the way Maugham begins his novel:

I have never begun a novel with more misgiving. If I call it a novel it is only because I don't know what else to call it. I have little story to tell and I end neither with a death nor a marriage. Death ends all things and so is the comprehensive conclusion of a story, but marriage finishes it very properly too and the sophisticated are ill-advised to sneer at what is by convention termed a happy ending. It is a sound instinct of the common people which persuades them that with this all that needs to be said is said. When male and female, after whatever vicissitudes you like, are at last brought together they have fulfilled their biological function and interest passes to the generation that is to come. But I leave my reader in the air. This book consists of my recollections of a man with whom I was thrown into close contact only at long intervals, and I have little knowledge of what happened to him in between. I suppose that by the exercise of invention I could fill the gaps plausibly enough and so make my narrative more

7. John Steinbeck, *The Pearl* (New York: The Viking Press, 1961), p. 1.

coherent; but I have no wish to do that. I only want to set down what I know of my own knowledge.[8]

In this opening passage for his novel, Maugham has deliberately limited the point of view of his narrator—he will be a minor character who sets down only what he knows "of his own knowledge." But what he tells us will result from Maugham's selection of material to develop the central character rather than from the necessity to develop the character of the narrator himself in any great depth. Contrast the opening of Maugham's novel with the opening of Saul Bellow's _Henderson the Rain King:_

What made me take this trip to Africa? There is no quick explanation. Things got worse and worse and worse and pretty soon they were too complicated.

When I think of my condition at the age of fifty-five when I bought the ticket, all is grief. The facts begin to crowd me and soon I get a pressure in the chest. A disorderly rush begins—my parents, my wives, my girls, my children, my farm, my animals, my habits, my money, my music lessons, my drunkenness, my prejudices, my brutality, my teeth, my face, my soul! I have to cry, "No, no, get back, curse you, let me alone!" But how can they let me alone? They belong to me. They are mine. And they pile into me from all sides. It turns into chaos.

However, the world which I thought so mighty an oppressor has removed its wrath from me. But if I am to make sense to you people and explain why I went to Africa I must face up to the facts.[9]

Maugham's narrator explains directly how he will tell his story, while Bellow's narrator only says he must "face up to the facts"—at the same time, however, implying a good deal about his method as storyteller from the very way in which he begins his story. Both novels, we will later find, recount the experiences of men in search of self-knowledge and self-realization in exotic and alien environments; but it is obvious from the opening of each novel that Maugham's narrator will be only a minor character looking in at the search from the outside, while Bellow's narrator will be the hero who undergoes the experiences he describes. Although both narrators are first-person rather than third-person, this distinction, as in most narratives, is not

8. W. Somerset Maugham, _The Razor's Edge_ (Garden City, N.Y.: Doubleday Company, Inc., 1944), p. 1.
9. Saul Bellow, _Henderson the Rain King_ (New York: The Viking Press, 1959), p. 3.

very useful, since it does not in itself tell us very much about the limitations of each narrator. The important thing to notice is the exact nature of the limitations in each case: in Maugham, the limitations come from the narrator's remaining outside the main character's mind and hence, of necessity, reporting from a distance; in Bellow, the limitations come from the narrator's confusion about his own motives, although he will tell his own story from the inside, remaining very close to it. In one case the limitation is a logical one imposed by the physical necessities of a particular point of view, while in the other the limitation is a psychological one imposed by the character and personality of the hero-narrator.

Intrusive vs. self-effacing. The distinction between omniscient and limited should not be confused with a related way of distinguishing between points of view of narrators—which is well illustrated in the following two passages, the first from a draft for *Madame Bovary,* the second from Flaubert's final version of that novel:

> There was no doubt that the dinner on the previous evening had been a big event in [Leon's] life, for his life up to that time had had very few events. The only son of a widow of no great wealth, who had sent him to school in a seminary at Yvetot, and later, for reasons of economy, to do his apprenticeship in a law office in Yonville, he had never before found himself in an intimate conversation with a lady for two full hours. But how had he suddenly been able to express, and witḥ such eloquence, all those confused matters which the evening before he would have had difficulty even formulating for himself? Is it that our hearts, like small pebbles, wait motionless in the spot where Providence has placed them, for the precise shock which will strike a spark? Or is it with them as with a broker's safe, that there exists between their mysterious hinges and certain words which one must know, a connecting spring which releases when it is touched so that the doors instantly open wide and the cash-filled drawers roll out of their own accord? He was reserved in his speech and usually maintained that silence about his own affairs appropriate to feminine natures, combining modesty with deceit. It was generally agreed at Yonville that his manners were distinguished, for he listened respectfully to the advice of his elders and did not seem too hot-headed in politics[,] something remarkable in a young man.[10]

10. Gustave Flaubert, *Madame Bovary: Backgrounds and Sources; Essays in Criticism,* Norton Critical Edition, ed. with a substantially new translation by Paul De Man (New York: W. W. Norton & Company, Inc., 1965), pp. 270–271.

The dinner of the evening before had been a considerable event for [Leon]; he had never till then talked for two hours consecutively to a "lady." How then had he been able to express, and in such language, so many things that he could not have said so well before? He was usually shy, and maintained that reserve which partakes at once of modesty and dissimulation. At Yonville, his manners were generally admired. He listened to the opinions of the older people, and seemed to have moderate political views, a rare thing for a young man.[11]

In both versions Flaubert's narrator is the omniscient author, though he chooses to tell us more in the first than in the second passage. But the most important difference between the two passages lies in the sorts of things the narrator tells us, rather than in the sheer quantity of information. In the first passage there is what we might call an *intrusive* narrator. He pauses to give us a good deal of background about Leon's education. More important, he speculates at length on the reasons for Leon's sudden ability to express himself and in the course of doing so, makes general speculations about life. He makes an observation about the combination of "modesty with deceit" which he feels is "appropriate to feminine natures." We sense that the narrator is standing between us and the story, making his presence felt in various ways and sometimes using his story as a starting point for comments on various topics which the story suggests. Sometimes, as in Fielding's novels, the intrusive narrator may even interrupt the progress of his story to insert little essays which are more or less self-contained.

In Flaubert's second passage, on the other hand, there is what we might call a *self-effacing* narrator. He gives us mainly facts and the opinions of others about Leon. He leaves us to speculate on how Leon was suddenly able to express himself so well. He simply describes him as shy with "that reserve which partakes at once of modesty and dissimulation," without adding the comment about its appropriateness "to feminine natures." We sense that the narrator is immersing himself in his story, but also, curiously enough, remaining as detached and objective as possible in his telling of it. Sometimes, as in many twentieth-century novels, the self-effacing narrator may efface himself so well that it is hard to detect his presence.

There is no single necessary correlation between these two ways of distinguishing points of view of narrators. Steinbeck's narrator in *The Pearl* is omniscient but self-effacing, since he assumes the stance of knowing everything he chooses to but at the same time does not

11. *Ibid.*, p. 61.

intrude his own comments about what he knows. Maugham's and Bellow's narrators adopt differing limitations in point of view, but both are intrusive narrators, injecting their own comments on the way they will tell their stories. And other combinations are possible.

In the first chapter of *Pride and Prejudice*, Jane Austen illustrates the omniscient-intrusive narrator. She begins the novel with a generalization, then reports a conversation between Mr. and Mrs. Bennet, and finally gives a summary of the traits of character that have been revealed by the conversation:

It is a truth universally acknowledged, that a single man in possession of a good fortune must be in want of a wife.

However little known the feelings or views of such a man may be on his first entering a neighborhood, this truth is so well fixed in the minds of the surrounding families, that he is considered as the rightful property of someone or other of their daughters.

"My dear Mr. Bennet," said his lady to him one day, "have you heard that Netherfield Park is let at last?"

Mr. Bennet replied that he had not. . . .

"Why, my dear, you must know, Mrs. Long says that Netherfield is taken by a young man of large fortune from the north of England; that he came down on Monday in a chaise and four to see the place, and was so much delighted with it, that he agreed with Mr. Morris immediately; that he is to take possession before Michaelmas, and some of his servants are to be in the house by the end of next week."

"What is his name?"

"Bingley."

"Is he married or single?"

"Oh! single, my dear, to be sure! A single man of large fortune; four or five thousand a year. What a fine thing for our girls!"

"How so? How can it affect them?"

"My dear Mr. Bennet," replied his wife, "how can you be so tiresome! You must know that I am thinking of his marrying one of them."

"Is that his design in settling here?"

"Design? nonsense, how can you talk so! But it is very likely that he may fall in love with one of them, and therefore you must visit him as soon as he comes."

"I see no occasion for that. . . ."

"But, my dear, you must indeed go and see Mr. Bingley when he comes into the neighborhood."

"It is more than I engage for, I assure you."

"But consider your daughters. Only think what an establishment it would be for one of them! Sir William and Lady Lucas are determined to go, merely on that account; for in general, you know, they visit no new-comers. Indeed you must go; for it will be impossible for us to visit him if you do not."

"You are over-scrupulous, surely. I dare say Mr. Bingley will be very glad to see you; and I will send a few lines by you to assure him of my hearty consent to his marrying whichever he chooses of the girls; though I must throw in a good word for my little Lizzy."

"I desire you will do no such thing. Lizzy is not a bit better than the others; and I am sure she is not half so handsome as Jane, nor half as good-humored as Lydia. But you are always giving her the preference."

"They have none of them much to recommend them," replied he: "they are all silly and ignorant, like other girls; but Lizzy has something more of quickness than her sisters."

"Mr. Bennet, how can you abuse your own children in such a way? You take delight in vexing me. You have no compassion on my poor nerves."

"You mistake me, my dear. I have a high respect for your nerves. They are my old friends. I have heard you mention them with consideration these twenty years at least. . . ."

Mr. Bennet was so odd a mixture of quick parts, sarcastic humor, reserve, and caprice, that the experience of three-and-twenty years had been insufficient to make his wife understand his character. Her mind was less difficult to develop. She was a woman of mean understanding, little information, and uncertain temper. When she was discontented, she fancied herself nervous. The business of her life was to get her daughters married; its solace was visiting and news.[12]

Jane Austen's narrator makes intrusions of two kinds. The opening two paragraphs of the novel quoted above are a different kind of intrusion from that in the last paragraph. The opening paragraphs have broad thematic concerns: they suggest what the world of this novel is going to be like (a world concerned with marriage and money), establish the attitude toward this world that the narrator will adopt (satirical and ironic), and imply how the reader is meant to react to the story that will be presented (with amusement at the irony and satire rather than with deadly seriousness or indignation). These intrusions serve a necessary purpose at the beginning of the novel in

---

12. Jane Austen, *Pride and Prejudice* (Boston: Little, Brown and Company, 1899), Ch. 1, pp. 5–9.

establishing a point of view and a desired response from the reader. The intrusions in the last paragraph do not serve such a purpose. All of the points made in summary of the characters of Mr. and Mrs. Bennet have already been illustrated through their conversation. Mr. Bennet's wit and sarcastic humor has been shown in his question about Bingley's "design" in settling at Netherfield and his tongue-in-cheek offer to send a letter giving his consent to Bingley's marrying "whichever he chooses of the girls." Mrs. Bennet's "mean understanding" has been illustrated in her failure to grasp the fact that Mr. Bennet is teasing her with these remarks. We don't have to be told that she "fancied herself nervous"—we have already inferred this from Mr. Bennet's remarks. Likewise, the limits of her world—arranging marriages for her daughters, visiting, and gossiping—have already been clearly established. But we do not object to the intrusions in the summary of the Bennets' characters, partly because we have already accepted the value of the other kind of intrusion in the first two paragraphs, and partly because we have become interested in the intrusive narrator, who has almost become a character in the story. Eighteenth- and nineteenth-century novelists often indulge in intrusions of this kind, apparently feeling a more intimate relationship with their readers than many twentieth-century novelists do. The earlier audiences had a more nearly equal interest in the tale and the omniscient teller than many twentieth-century readers would, though most readers today still appreciate the wit and perception of the intrusions in these first two paragraphs of *Pride and Prejudice*.

In contrast, Ernest Hemingway, more typical of the twentieth century, chooses a narrator in *A Farewell to Arms* whose point of view is both limited and self-effacing. The story is told by an "I"—Lieutenant Frederick Henry—and this "I," though he reveals something about his own character by the way he tells the story, does not usually intrude with his own comments or interpretation; he simply uses his consciousness as a means of conveying to the reader what an objective observer might see. Here is a brief scene early in the book which helps to establish the characters of both Henry and Catherine Barkley, the British nurse at the Italian front during World War I whom Lieutenant Henry has just met. He has seen her once and learned that her fiancé has just been killed—and during this first meeting, Catherine, under the stress of the wartime situation, has hinted that she is falling in love with Henry, though he has not yet reciprocated. Unable to visit her for two days, Henry then comes to see her:

> We were off the driveway, walking under the trees. I took her hands, then stopped and kissed her.

"Isn't there anywhere we can go?"

"No," she said. "We have to just walk here. You've been away a long time."

"This is the third day. But I'm back now."

She looked at me, "And you do love me?"

"Yes."

"You did say you loved me, didn't you?"

"Yes," I lied. "I love you." I had not said it before. . . .

"I love you so and it's been awful. You won't go away?"

"No. I'll always come back."

"Oh, I love you so. . . ."

[Henry kisses Catherine, thinking she is "probably a little crazy," and knowing that he is not in love with her.] This was a game, like bridge, in which you said things instead of playing cards. Like bridge you had to pretend you were playing for money or playing for some stakes. Nobody had mentioned what the stakes were. It was all right with me. . . .

She looked down at the grass.

"This is a rotten game we play, isn't it?"

"What game?"

"Don't be dull."

"I'm not, on purpose."

"You're a nice boy," she said. "And you play it as well as you know how. But it's a rotten game."

"Do you always know what people think?"

"Not always. But I do with you. You don't have to pretend you love me. That's over for the evening. Is there anything you'd like to talk about?"

"But I do love you."

"Please let's not lie when we don't have to. I had a very fine little show and I'm all right now. . . ."[13]

Though Henry is a limited rather than an omniscient narrator, he manages to convey as full an understanding of the scene as an omniscient narrator could—largely, of course, through his reported conversation with Catherine. He learns more about Catherine's perceptions at the same time that we do—and her comments about him that he reports help to give us a better picture of him than we would gain through soliloquy or summary of his own thoughts alone. The main difference between Jane Austen's omniscient-intrusive narrator and Hemingway's limited-self-effacing narrator is not in the

13. Ernest Hemingway, *A Farewell to Arms* (New York: Charles Scribner's Sons, 1929, 1957), Ch. 6, pp. 31–32.

amount or kind of information that can be conveyed to the reader, but rather in the relationship between reader and narrator which is established. The reader is implicitly invited to share and accept the perspective of Jane Austen's omniscient narrator; he is implicitly invited to share Frederick Henry's limited perspective, but not necessarily to accept it without modification.

Authoritative vs. naive. This leads us to a further way of distinguishing between narrators' points of view. As has been said, we are obviously meant to take the interpretation of Mr. and Mrs. Bennet's characters given by Jane Austen's narrator as final truth; Frederick Henry's statements about Catherine are not meant to be taken in the same way. He will learn more about Catherine, just as we will, during the progress of the novel, and his perceptions about her will always be subject to the limitations imposed by the way he is characterized—the kind of values he has, the kind of consciousness he represents. An omniscient narrator may also have limitations in his values or his consciousness, but we, as readers, will be expected to accept these limitations while we read the book. A narrator with a limited point of view has standing behind him an author whose perspectives are usually broader than those of his characters. In other words, some narrators we accept as *authoritative,* others we see to one degree or another as *naive.* Jane Austen's authoritative narrator in the passage above is telling us at the very beginning of the novel what we should believe about Mr. and Mrs. Bennet during our reading of the entire novel (though, of course, we may find minor qualifications and modifications as we read on); Hemingway's naive narrator is telling us in the first part of the passage what to believe at that point about Catherine, though both he and we have significantly modified our conception of her character before we come to the end of the passage, and we will presumably change our perspective as we read on, agreeing or disagreeing with his developing insights. Thus the authoritative narrator starts with a fund of reliable knowledge which he gradually discloses to us; the naive narrator tells us what he believes to be the truth at any given moment.

But the distinction between authoritative and naive narrators is not quite so simple. In some kinds of fiction, for example, where consistency resides not so much in character and event as in overall idea or philosophy, there are switches from authoritative to naive that seem to violate consistency. Thus in *Gulliver's Travels* we see Gulliver sometimes as an authoritative narrator (expressing Swift's point of view) and sometimes as a naive narrator (serving as the object of Swift's satire). Contrast the attitudes of Gulliver as narrator in the following two passages. In the first, taken from Part One, he has just saved the kingdom of Lilliput from a naval invasion by the kingdom of Blefuscu, but refuses to pursue the war further:

> His majesty desired I would take some other opportunity of bringing all the rest of his enemy's ships into his ports. And so unmeasureable is the ambition of princes, that he seemed to think of nothing less than reducing the whole empire of Blefuscu into a province, and governing it by a viceroy . . . by which he would remain the sole monarch of the whole world. But I endeavoured to divert him from this design, by many arguments drawn from the topics of policy as well as justice; and I plainly protested, "that I would never be an instrument of bringing a free and brave people into slavery."[14]

In the second passage, taken from Part Two, Gulliver offers exactly the same kind of help to the King of Brobdingnag that he has refused to the emperor of Lilliput:

> In hopes to ingratiate my self farther into his majesty's favour, I told him of an invention, discovered between three and four hundred years ago, to make a certain powder, into a heap of which, the smallest spark of fire falling, would kindle the whole in a moment . . . and make it all fly up in the air together, with a noise and agitation greater than thunder. That a proper quantity of this powder rammed into an hollow tube . . . would drive a ball of iron or lead, with such violence and speed, as nothing was able to sustain its force. . . . That we often put this powder into large hollow balls of iron, and discharged them by an engine into some city we were besieging, which would rip up the pavements, tear the houses to pieces, burst and throw splinters on every side, dashing out the brains of all who came near. That I knew the ingredients very well . . . I understood the manner of compounding them, and could direct his workmen [so that he could] batter down the walls of the strongest town in his dominions in a few hours, or destroy the whole metropolis, if ever it should pretend to dispute his absolute commands. . . . The king was struck with horror at the description I had given of these terrible engines, and the proposal I had made. He was amazed, how so impotent and groveling an insect as I . . . could entertain such inhuman ideas. . . . As for himself, he protested, that . . . he would rather lose half his kingdom, than be privy to such a secret; which

14. Jonathan Swift, *Gulliver's Travels,* in *Classic Tales* (London: George Bell and Sons, 1885), Pt. 1, p. 324.

he commanded me, as I valued my life, never to mention any more.[15]

Gulliver's Travels achieves consistency in its point of view through Swift's underlying philosophy and attitudes rather than through the narrator. In the first passage quoted above, Swift's views are expressed by Gulliver, in the second, by the King of Brobdingnag as Gulliver seems to reverse himself. This reversal works within the context of the book because we sense that Swift makes Gulliver sometimes the authoritative narrator and sometimes the naive narrator for the sake of a larger satirical purpose in which characters are used as devices for expressing ideas. We recognize this larger purpose because of the way Swift builds up the whole design of his book—and perhaps we are also more ready to accept the seeming inconsistency in Gulliver's changing points of view because human beings in real life may act inconsistently, behaving differently in different contexts. In one sense, then, the narrator with a strictly consistent point of view is more characteristic of art than of life.

Implications for teaching

Let us pause for a moment and consider some implications for teaching narratives that are implicit in the distinctions we have been making. It should have become clear that understanding the point of view of the narrator is crucial for understanding the other elements in a story, but that merely to identify the point of view in a given narrative as first or third person or as limited or omniscient is not very useful. Students should be led to assess the specific limitations and opportunities provided by a point of view and to appreciate its advantages and disadvantages. They should recognize the significance of their own reactions to a narrator in determining their attitude toward a story and its characters and events. There are at least three specific problems of special importance that the teacher faces in helping students to understand narrators and their significance in stories.

First, there is the problem that the omniscient-intrusive narrator may seem a little old-fashioned to students today. Having grown up in a generation that has seen the virtues of seeming objectivity in writers like Hemingway and Salinger, they may wonder what right authors like Fielding and Dickens have to intrude into the stories they are telling, thus interrupting the action. Teachers can, of course, explain the omniscient-intrusive narrator-author as a historical phenomenon,

15. *Ibid.,* Pt. 2, pp. 402–403.

but this is not enough. Through asking the same kinds of questions about an intrusive author-narrator that one might ask about a character, the teacher can lead students to an interest in the narrator's personality and viewpoints. In talking about the opening of *Pride and Prejudice,* for example, the teacher can arouse an interest in the wry comments of Jane Austen's author-narrator by pointing to clues in the language itself (e.g., "must be in want of a wife," "considered as the rightful property") which establish that point of view.

The second problem lies in interpreting what a self-effacing narrator tells us and in filling in any necessary gaps. In the passage from *A Farewell to Arms* quoted above, for example, what are we to make of Frederick Henry and of Catherine? Is Catherine "a little crazy," as Frederick suggests? At this point in the novel will male readers be likely to identify with Frederick, female readers with Catherine, and apportion their sympathies accordingly? Will the standards of morality and the concepts about human relationships held by an individual reader influence his interpretation of what the self-effacing narrator says? And is the attitude of Hemingway, the author, different from that of Frederick Henry, the narrator? Asking questions like these, teacher and class can work toward a better understanding of the preparation in these early scenes of the novel for the later unfolding of a love story which begins completely casually for Henry and very suddenly and intensely for Catherine.

The third problem lies in judging how authoritative or reliable a narrator is. In *Gulliver's Travels* the situation itself is so far removed from the surface realities of life that the reader is likely to be prevented from a complete identification with Gulliver and hence will perhaps be more apt to focus on what happens to Gulliver than on the character of Gulliver himself. The seeming inconsistency between the two passages quoted above may thus not be so noticeable. But in a book like *The Catcher in the Rye,* adolescent readers especially will be likely to identify strongly with Holden Caulfield, and though it is his story, they should realize that his point of view has some limitations. If he had told the story as an adult narrator looking back on his youth (as Gene Forrester does in John Knowles' *A Separate Peace*), it would have been a different story, and students might be asked to speculate on what those differences might have been.[16] Such speculation is invited by the ending of *The Catcher in the Rye,* since Holden confesses that he doesn't know how to assess what has happened to him. As students are asked to decide what *they* think about it, they will inevitably come to grips with the question of how reliable Holden is as a narrator and be led to consider character, motive, and theme.

---

16. For Knowles' remarks about *A Separate Peace* see p. 147–155 below.

Another way of looking at these three problems is to say that students must understand work, writer, and reader as they read any book. As they distinguish between omniscient and limited narrators and assess the limitations of any point of view, they will focus on the work, determining how much we see of the world and the particular situation which it presents. As they distinguish between intrusive and self-effacing narrators, they will concentrate on the writer and determine how much he comments on the story he tells, either directly as author-narrator or indirectly through a narrator who is a character. As they make distinctions between the authoritative and the naive narrator, they will be concentrating on themselves as readers, trying to determine how much they should believe of what they are told and how to interpret those things related by a narrator that lie somewhere on the boundary of credibility.

The worlds of fiction

As noted above, any narrative has two elements: a narrator and a stream of events in the past, recollected or imagined. Just as it is important for students to be aware of who the narrator is and how he has chosen to tell his story, it is also important for them to understand the nature of the stream of events and the kind of world in which those events take place.

Imaginary world vs. real world. First of all, let us establish the extremes or limits of possible worlds. At one extreme, there are the stories that take place in an *imaginary world.* They begin, explicitly or implicitly, with "Once upon a time . . . ." These are the fairy stories which children first come to love; they are narratives of escape that adults relax with; but they may also be satires, accounts of utopias, works of science fiction, or allegories. They include both the *Odyssey* and *Gulliver's Travels,* both *1984* and Spenser's *Faerie Queene* and *Pilgrim's Progress* and *Rasselas* and *Candide.* They are the books in which ideas, or the author's imaginative manipulation of a hypothesis or an unusual situation, take precedence over people and events of the real world as we know it. They make no real claim to historical fact (though, like the *Odyssey,* they may have some historical basis). At the other extreme are *histories:* real ones like *Hiroshima,* or imagined ones like *The Red Badge of Courage, A Farewell to Arms,* or *A Tale of Two Cities.* Along with histories are biographies and autobiographies, real or feigned: Boswell's *Life of Johnson,* Franklin's *Autobiography, Tom Jones, Great Expectations,* and *David Copperfield,* and (in spite of what Holden Caulfield says to the contrary) *The Catcher in the Rye.* These are the books in which the author's allegiance to the real world—its unique or its typical events, its people, its look and feel—is paramount. Idea and imagination are, of course, important in these books, but ideas take shape out of the real world, and the author's imagination is bounded by the limits of that world.

This last point deserves further discussion. Streams of events taking place in an imaginary world obviously can be seen as relevant to the real world, either through a process of intellectual abstraction or through immediate intuition. Books with streams of events taking place in the real world may fail to reflect relevant and important things about that world, or may reflect the world unconvincingly, although they do not demand the imaginative leap to perceive relevance (or the lack of it) that the other kind of book demands. And there are some books that may appear to belong to one world while actually belonging to the other—since the imaginary world will be most appealing if it has an air of verisimilitude about it, and the real world will strike us as most dramatic and interesting if it has been given an intensity and concentration that are not necessarily found in life. Skillful writers may thus manage to have something of the best of both worlds in a book, though the book will belong basically to one world or the other, as in the illustrations which follow. In the opening sentences of *Animal Farm,* a book in which an imaginary world is created, notice how carefully George Orwell manages the jump into that world from the real world:

> Mr. Jones, of the Manor Farm, had locked the hen-houses for the night, but was too drunk to remember to shut the popholes. With the ring of light from his lantern dancing from side to side, he lurched across the yard, kicked off his boots at the back door, drew himself a last glass of beer from the barrel in the scullery, and made his way up to bed, where Mrs. Jones was already snoring.
>
> As soon as the light in the bedroom went out there was a stirring and a fluttering all through the farm buildings. Word had gone round during the day that old Major, the prize Middle White boar, had had a strange dream on the previous night and wished to communicate it to the other animals.[17]

The details of the first paragraph, thoroughly consistent with the real world, prepare us for a smooth leap into the imaginary world of the animals in the second paragraph, and this kind of realistic detail enriches the entire story and helps us to maintain our interest in the imaginary world throughout. Contrast with this the opening para-

17. George Orwell, *Animal Farm* (New York: Harcourt Brace Jovanovich, Inc., 1946), p. 3.

graph of E. M. Forster's *A Passage to India,* a story which is to take place in an unfamiliar corner of the real world that Forster has lived in, knows well, and will fictionalize only slightly:

> Except for the Marabar Caves—and they are twenty miles off— the city of Chandrapore presents nothing extraordinary. Edged rather than washed by the river Ganges, it trails for a couple of miles along the bank, scarcely distinguishable from the rubbish it deposits so freely. There are no bathing-steps on the river front, as the Ganges happens not to be holy here; indeed there is no river front, and bazaars shut out the wide and shifting panorama of the stream. The streets are mean, the temples ineffective, and though a few fine houses exist they are hidden away in gardens or down alleys whose filth deters all but the invited guest. Chandrapore was never large or beautiful, but two hundred years ago it lay on the road between Upper India, then imperial, and the sea, and the fine houses date from that period. The zest for decoration stopped in the eighteenth century, nor was it ever democratic. There is no painting and scarcely any carving in the bazaars. The very wood seems made of mud, the inhabitants of mud moving. So abased, so monotonous is everything that meets the eye, that when the Ganges comes down it might be expected to wash the excrescence back into the soil. Houses do fall, people are drowned and left rotting, but the general outline of the town persists, swelling here, shrinking there, like some low but indestructible form of life.[18]

The real world of this novel is more exotic, more remote from everyday life, in some ways, than is the imaginary world of *Animal Farm.* Forster, like Orwell, gives details—the bazaars, the streets, the temples, the houses, the alleys, the filth, the river. But here the details are used not so much to create an air of verisimilitude as to heighten reality. All the details are arranged and subordinated in such a way as to contribute to the overall imaginative perception of the setting Forster is attempting to convey—the "abased" and "monotonous" scene in which "the very wood seems made of mud, the inhabitants of mud moving."

Inner world vs. outer world. The distinction between real and imaginary worlds should not be confused with a related one, that between the *inner psychological world* and the *outer world of action.* Though some books may belong almost exclusively to one or the

18. E. M. Forster, *A Passage to India* (New York: Harcourt Brace Jovanovich, Inc., 1924, 1952), p. 7.

other of these, many books move back and forth between the inner
action taking place in characters' minds and the outer actions taking
place around them. Such a movement between the real and the
imaginary worlds would not normally be possible. Sometimes an
author may show the inner and outer worlds almost at the same time.
Take, for example, the scene from James Joyce's *A Portrait of the
Artist as a Young Man* in which Joyce's hero, Stephen Dedalus, is on
his way to his classes at the university:

> It must be eleven, he thought, and peered into a dairy to see the
> time. The clock in the dairy told him that it was five minutes to
> five but, as he turned away, he heard a clock somewhere near
> him, but unseen, beating eleven strokes in swift precision. . . .
> Eleven! Then he was late for that lecture too. What day of the
> week was it? He stopped at a newsagent's to read the headline of
> a placard. Thursday. Ten to eleven, English; eleven to twelve,
> French; twelve to one, physics. He fancied to himself the English
> lecture and felt, even at that distance, restless and helpless. He
> saw the heads of his classmates meekly bent as they wrote in
> their notebooks the points they were bidden to note, nominal
> definitions, essential definitions and examples or dates of birth or
> death, chief works, a favourable and an unfavourable criticism
> side by side. His own head was unbent for his thoughts wandered
> abroad and whether he looked around the little class of students
> or out of the window across the desolate gardens of the green an
> odour assailed him of cheerless cellardamp and decay.[19]

By presenting the inner and outer worlds simultaneously, Joyce is able
to show us both how Stephen's mind works and how he reacts to the
world around him. His daydreaming shows his "restless and helpless"
state of mind at this point in the novel. The juxtaposition of inner and
outer worlds contributes to the development of both character and
theme.

Fast action vs. slow action. Whether events take place in the inner
or the outer world, in a real or an imaginary world, they may be
presented summarily or in detail through what we might call *fast
action* or *slow action.* Consider the amount of action covered in this
single sentence from the end of the first part of Defoe's *Robinson
Crusoe.* Crusoe is telling the story:

> In the meantime, I in part settled myself here; for, first of all, I

19. James Joyce, *A Portrait of the Artist as a Young Man* (New York: The Viking Press, 1916, 1964),
Ch. V, pp. 177–178.

married, and that not either to my disadvantage or dissatisfaction, and had three children, two sons and one daughter; but my wife dying, and my nephew coming home with good success from a voyage to Spain, my inclination to go abroad, and his importunity, prevailed, and engaged me to go in his ship as a private trader to the East Indies. This was in the year 1694.[20]

Contrast with this a passage a scant ten pages earlier in which Crusoe describes his man Friday's fight with a bear:

But never was a fight managed so hardily, and in such a surprising manner, as that which followed between Friday and the bear, which gave us all, though at first we were surprised and afraid for him, the greatest diversion imaginable. As the bear is a heavy, clumsy creature, and does not gallop as the wolf does, who is swift and light, so he has two particular qualities, which generally are the rule of his actions: first, as to men, who are not his proper prey . . . he does not usually attempt them, unless they first attack him. On the contrary, if you meet him in the woods, if you do not meddle with him, he won't meddle with you; but then you must take care to be very civil to him and give him the road, for he is a very nice gentleman. He won't go a step out of his way for a prince; nay, if you are really afraid, your best way is to look another way, and keep going on; for sometimes if you stop, and stand still, and look steadily at him, he takes it for an affront; but if you throw or toss anything at him, and it hits him, though it were but a bit of a stick as big as your finger, he takes it for an affront, and sets all his other business aside to pursue his revenge; for he will have satisfaction in point of honour. That is his first quality; the next is, that if he be once affronted, he will never leave you, night or day, till he has his revenge, but follows, at a good round rate, till he overtakes you. . . .

[O]n a sudden, we spied the bear come out of the wood, and a vast monstrous one it was, the biggest by far that ever I saw. We were all a little surprised when we saw him; but when Friday saw him, it was easy to see joy and courage in the fellow's countenance. "O! O! O!" says Friday, three times pointing to him. "O master! you give me te leave; me shakee te hand with him; me make you good laugh."

Friday throws a stone at the bear and gets the bear to follow him up a tree. Crusoe continues:

20. Daniel Defoe, *Robinson Crusoe* (London: J. M. Dent and Company, 1899), p. 341.

When we came to the tree, there was Friday got out to the small end of a large limb of the tree, and the bear got about half way to him. As soon as the bear got out to that part where the limb of the tree was weaker, "Ha!" says he to us, "now you see me teachee the bear dance." So he falls a-jumping and shaking the bough, at which the bear began to totter, but stood still, and began to look behind him, to see how he should get back. Then, indeed, we did laugh heartily. But Friday had not done with him by a great deal. When he sees him stand still, he calls out to him again, as if he had supposed the bear could speak English, "What, you no come farther? pray you come farther"; so he left jumping and shaking the tree; and the bear, just as if he had understood what he said, did come a little farther; then he fell a-jumping again, and the bear stopped again.[21]

The account of the incident continues for another three paragraphs before Friday finally shoots and kills the bear. Defoe, like many other authors, sometimes covers the events of several years in a sentence and sometimes takes several paragraphs or several pages for the events of a few minutes.

Implications for teaching

Let us pause again and consider some implications for teaching narratives that are implicit in what we have been saying about the stream of events. It is obviously not enough for students to merely know what happens: they must understand the causes behind events, and indeed their definition of what constitutes an event may need to be stretched. Most books will have a blend of fast and slow action, but the proportions of that blend are significant, both generically and qualitatively. A book with all fast action is not able to look very deeply at its characters, nor to explore the significance of what they do, the chains of motivation and cause and effect that lead to and away from particular actions, nor is it likely to deal with the inner world at all. In many ways the history of the novel reflects a development of the uses of slow action, a moving away from the mere "action" or "adventure" story toward a more complex and ultimately more rewarding kind of art. Complexity in the text, however, demands sophistication in the reader; and part of the job of the teacher of fiction is to help students move from simpler to more complex texts and from the simpler pleasures provided by fast action, taking place largely in the outer

21. *Ibid.*, pp. 327–328, 330.

world, to the more complex pleasures of slow action, which often moves back and forth between the outer and inner worlds. In working toward this goal of increasing the understanding and enjoyment of adolescent readers, the teacher may face at least three problems in connection with the stream of events in a narrative.

The first problem is simply to get students to interpret and accept events in the perspective of the world which the author has created. The student who is too literal-minded may dismiss the world of *Gulliver's Travels* as farfetched and ridiculous; the student who demands complete "realism" may object to the heightening of reality in the excerpt from *A Passage to India* quoted above. The teacher must lead the student to see that a book may be meaningful and pleasurable in a number of ways. Some novels ask a reader to immerse himself in events and to experience the same reactions to those events that the characters do. Others—like *Gulliver*—demand a certain amount of detachment and a commitment that is more intellectual than emotional. Students must come to think of "identification" with a book as placing themselves in its world as well as placing it in theirs. The teacher can help them to achieve this double perspective through questions that ask students to look at the details of the particular world of a particular book before moving on to questions that call for comparison with their own world.

The second problem is to make the inner world as exciting for students as the outer world. Naive readers will often be bored by a book in which there is much less outer action than inner action. Here the teacher needs to enlarge students' concepts of what an event is. He must lead students to see that the writer can dramatize choice and mental struggle so that they are as exciting as events in the outer world. He must lead better students, at least, to see that the act of perception itself can be as exciting as any overt act. In the passage from *A Farewell to Arms* quoted above, for example, the fact that Frederick Henry kisses Catherine is not as interesting as the reason why he does so and Catherine's instinctive understanding of that reason.

The third problem, related to the second, is to make slow action interesting. The naive reader who complains that "nothing happens" in a book with slow action must be led to see that actually a great deal happens, but that to understand the significance of what happens and to enable us to really know the characters, the author has chosen a slower pace and at the same time given us a more complete picture. At least mild dissatisfaction with a book that has only fast action might be created by asking searching questions that the author has left unanswered about people and events: How does the character look? Where is he and what does the place look like? Why did he do this? How did other people feel when he did it? The dissatisfaction can then be put to use in creating acceptance for a more difficult book, containing more slow action, which answers questions like these.

To repeat, the theoretical framework for analyzing the basic components of narrative that has been set up will have value for the teacher only if he can translate theory into classroom practices that will make students more discerning readers. If the teacher is to help his students become better readers, he must make choices about what students should read as well as choices about how to guide students in their reading. He must have a philosophy about curriculum and an understanding of the reading process.

Curriculum planning. As has been pointed out, most people begin their acquaintance with narrative when very young and the interest in narratives of one sort or another is likely to remain throughout life. In planning curriculums, teachers have often tended to overlook this continuum and have neglected to make bridges between the reading done for school assignments and that done on students' own impulses. This neglect has sprung, I believe, from two assumptions: first, that differences in quality between books read in school and some of those read outside of school prevent one from relating the two; and second, that the teacher's role in guiding student reading is to talk *about* literature—or even about the backgrounds which produce it—rather than to help students toward richer experiences in reading itself. As a consequence, in many curriculums one finds two movements in the sequence from one grade level to the next. There is an entirely appropriate movement from simpler to more sophisticated kinds of narrative; but there is also an inappropriate movement from the more direct experience with narrative in elementary and junior high school to the study of criticism in the senior high school without the engagement with narrative itself.

John Dixon, reporting on discussions at the Dartmouth Seminar, reminds us that "the principle of organization of a critical statement is cognitive; that of a work of literature is, in the final analysis, affective"; and although "it is much easier to teach literary criticism than to teach literature," the teaching of literature should be our primary job. This means that the student should be led to take account of both the work and his reaction to it. The process of reading is most successful, Dixon says, when the student can say, "That's me!" as he reads. *"That's me,"* Dixon continues, "has two components, and our aim is to move dynamically from the *me* of personal identification to the *that* of the [work of literature]. The discipline lies in the attention to the *that,* and it should be made plain that there is no real dichotomy here, but a natural movement from subject to object and back again. The *That's me* may reveal a very partial and too selective attention to the work, but the teacher will get nowhere in the attempt to make the work meaningful if he does not begin with the *me.*"[22] Though this might imply that we should teach only narratives with which students may identify directly from their own past experience, I believe we need not conceive of 'the *me* so narrowly. Adolescents will not necessarily respond to a book about their own world if it seems false to them, nor will they fail to respond to books about other worlds— provided these are within their understanding (though not within their experience) and are presented so that they seem coherent and interesting.

Whether the experience of narrative will seem coherent and interesting depends in large part, of course, upon the book itself; but it also depends upon the ways in which the teacher guides the experience of reading. The teacher can draw implications from the theoretical framework developed earlier in this chapter to guide that experience. As students move from less sophisticated to more sophisticated kinds of narrative, many of the basic questions that the teacher asks should remain the same, though they should be couched in different terms and presented in different contexts. At any level the effort should be to make clear the relationship between the *that* and the *me.*

If the *that* and the *me* are to be drawn together, students must identify the work with their experience or their interests. This can be best accomplished by sequences of questions that move from "What?" to "Why?" The *what* on its simplest level has to do with the stream of events that constitute the narrative: it means simply knowing what happens. But one cannot fully understand what happens without understanding why it happens, and this involves cause and effect relationships, motives of characters, and the impact of social forces. More than this, it means an understanding of the role of the narrator and the development of point of view. Thus questions should begin with the facts of what happens but move quickly to include the causes and motives behind the facts, the reasons for the way the story has been presented to us, and the narrator's attitude toward it.

Different kinds of reading. If students are to ask and answer these different kinds of questions and hence profit most from the books they read, they must develop increasing versatility in the way they read. Teachers must recognize that we read different kinds of things for different purposes and in different manners. Donald Hall—poet,

---

22. John Dixon, *Growth Through English* (Reading, England: National Association for the Teaching of English, 1967), pp. 59–60. Dixon mingles his own comments with those of Seminar participant Barbara Hardy.

critic, and teacher—makes useful distinctions among four kinds of reading. The first, Hall says, is "reading for information," the kind of reading we do when we read a newspaper, a set of directions, or most textbooks. We read quickly, paying attention only to the facts we need to gather and ignoring the language in which they are presented, "the rhythm of the sentence, or the play of metaphor." The second kind of reading, "reading literature," (or "literary reading," as I shall call it for convenience' sake) is an altogether different activity. We hear the sounds of words and perceive the rhythms of sentences as we read; we "also register a track of feeling through the metaphors and associations of words." "Careless writing," Hall says, "prevents this sort of attention and becomes offensive. But the great writers reward it. Only by the full exercise of our powers to receive language can we absorb their intelligence and their imagination. This kind of reading goes through the ear—though the eye takes in the print and decodes it into sound—to the throat and the understanding, and it can never be quick. It is slow and sensual, a deep pleasure that begins with touch and ends with the sort of comprehension that we associate with dream." The third kind of reading, "intellectual reading," is too often substituted for the second in the reading of literature, Hall believes. Intellectual reading is reading "in order to reduce images to abstractions." It is slow and "much time must be spent with the eyes turned away from the pages, reflecting on the text. To read literature this way," Hall says, "is to turn it into something it is not—to concepts clothed in character, or philosophy sugar-coated." It is to "miss literature completely" and concern oneself "with a minor discipline called the history of ideas." The fourth kind of reading, "narcotic reading," is "the automated daydream, the mild trip of the housewife and the tired businessman interested not in experience and feeling but in turning off the possibilities of experience and feeling." It is not "a window on the world [but] a screen against it." "Great literature," Hall says, "if we read it well, opens us up to the world and makes us more sensitive to it, as if we had acquired eyes that could see through things and ears that could hear smaller sounds. But, by narcotic reading, one can reduce great literature. . . . One can read *Anna Karenina* passively and inattentively and float down the river of lethargy as if one were reading a confession magazine: 'I Spurned My Husband for a Count.'"[23]

As Hall suggests, there are different ways to read and misread literature. He believes that everyone engages in narcotic reading occasionally, and "perhaps most consistently in late adolescence,

23. Donald Hall, "Four Kinds of Reading," *New York Times Book Review*, January 26, 1969, pp. 2, 30.

when great readers are born." I think one might amend his statement to include earlier adolescence as well; and if this is true, teachers can take advantage of this tendency, both in the books they select for students to read and in the way they approach those books, in order to first develop a love of reading and then gradually lead students toward the more demanding "literary reading." In both narcotic reading and literary reading, students' imaginations are involved. In both, reading becomes an experience rather than a chore: but the nature and results of the experience are sharply different. In one case the reader escapes into another world; in the other, he develops new insights into his own world. But these insights should come as the result of the experience itself of literary reading rather than as the end product of "intellectual reading." Too often we are tempted to teach literature through intellectual reading alone: to wean students from the Hardy boys in order to prepare them to discuss determinism versus free will in *Lord of the Flies.* Golding's novel does raise abstract philosophical issues; but it also tells an exciting and compelling story about a group of boys who are living beings engaging in exciting actions that are actually more interesting than those of the Hardy boys. In the interview in Part Five, John Knowles makes essentially the same point:

> I think a novel should be taken at face value first—as an experience. And then you might go on to the reverberations. You start with a very special concrete set of people and experiences. That is, in the first instance, what counts. And it is the primary value of my books anyway. Then, if you want to go on into the underlying reverberations and themes as secondary values, fine. But it's important to keep that order straight.[24]

Knowles might at first glance appear to advocate literary reading first, to be followed by "intellectual reading." But if one starts with the concrete set of people and experiences, then discussion of the "reverberations" will grow naturally out of earlier discussion of character, motive, and event. This is very different from "intellectual reading," in which one tries to bypass the narrative and its participants in order to arrive as quickly as possible at philosophical and thematic implications.

Knowles recognizes another side to the novel besides its story. In the earlier history of the novel, he says, readers were interested in its "informational side." They read novels partly "for such things as the

24. See p. 149 below.

picture of Dickens' London."[25] This is not necessarily the same thing as Hall's first kind of reading, reading for information, because presumably the information about Dickens' London is more complete and more satisfying if one grasps the nuances of Dickens' style and pays attention to his language. One would read an atlas or a geography or history textbook for information; one would read a chapter from Dickens describing London in some manner halfway between Hall's first and second kinds of reading. The important point to make, however, is that reading a novel for information is one of the possible reasons for reading novels, and the information a student gathers may be another way of striking his interest. Any novel which has a rich texture in its description of scene or milieu has potentially that interest. Hence students should not be discouraged, especially at the beginning of their reading careers, from this kind of reading. *A Tale of Two Cities* tells us a great deal of interesting information about the French Revolution, and this may be the first thing to catch some readers' interests. It is legitimate for the teacher to capitalize on those interests while at the same time leading students to appreciate other things about the book as well. Helping students to read fiction intelligently means helping them to achieve more versatility in their reading skills, and above all to develop the skill of literary reading.

Summary

Although we have emphasized throughout this Part that each kind of narrative makes its own special demands upon a reader and that each individual work must be approached on its own terms, we may summarize a few general principles that a teacher might keep in mind in teaching any narrative:

1. *Help students first to understand what goes on but then to move to causes; in other words, move from "What?" to "Why?"* Even very young readers who may need a good deal of guidance in sorting out chronology and determining exactly what happens will not be fully interested in a story until they are led to understand why characters act as they do and what the significance of those actions is.

2. *Be aware of what happens to adolescent readers as they read.* This means, first of all, helping students understand things that are likely to give them difficulty. It also means spotting those stories and those particular moments in stories in which students are most apt to

_____
25. See p. 153 below.

identify with character and situation and then determining how to take advantage of the identification without distorting the students' understanding of the story itself. It means finding ways to maintain their interest in those stories which invite detachment rather than direct identification. Finally, it means helping students to become more aware of their own process of reading.

3. *Help students toward a clearer understanding of the point of view of the narrator.* Lead them beyond the mere classification into first or third person point of view to an understanding of the advantages, limitations, and consequences of a particular point of view in a particular story. Help them to distinguish between authoritative and naive narrators, to fill in the gaps a self-effacing narrator inevitably leaves, to regard the intrusive narrator as almost another character in his story and hence as potentially worthy of interest rather than merely a representative of an old-fashioned technique.

4. *Help students to enter the world of each work.* This means helping them understand the differences between imaginary and real, and inner and outer worlds, and using that understanding to avoid out-of-hand rejection of a world which is not their own because it is not "realistic." It also means helping them to see correspondences between unfamiliar worlds and their own, again without distorting the total meaning or significance of a book.

5. *Help students to develop their taste.* This means helping them to work with increasingly complex texts in order to achieve increasingly sophisticated pleasures from their reading. It may mean helping them to move from books which contain mainly fast action to books in which this is mixed with slow action and in which there is fuller development of character, motive, and theme. It may mean simply helping them to become more versatile readers and to know what kind of reading is appropriate for a particular text. It will mean challenging them to read more difficult but potentially more satisfying books than they are reading, whatever their present levels may be.

6. *Avoid the extremes of teaching narrative from a purely didactic, a purely experiential, or a purely aesthetic point of view; but at the same time help students toward an understanding of theme, relation of what they read to their own lives, and appreciation of narrative patterns.* In other words, don't teach narratives as embodiments of simplistic moral lessons, but rather as expressions of complex and sometimes ambiguous views about human life. Teach them as significant to

students' own lives, but often indirectly and obliquely so. Teach them as composed of plot and pattern, but as containing more than these, with patterns contributing to theme. Finally, teach narratives as wholes, as works in which a student's maximum pleasure can come only from the perception of the meeting of pattern, theme, and significance to himself.

PART THREE

The Many Worlds of Huckleberry Finn

"One element in the greatness of *Huckleberry Finn*," Lionel Trilling asserts, "is that it succeeds first as a boy's book. One can read it at ten and then annually ever after, and each year find that it is as fresh as the year before, that it has changed only in becoming larger. To read it young," he concludes, "is like planting a tree young—each year adds a new growth-ring of meaning, and the book is as little likely as the tree to become dull."[1] Perhaps today's often reluctant readers can hardly be expected to reread any book year after year, but it is nonetheless true that Twain's book is unusual both in the number of different levels of meaning which readers can grasp at different stages in their development and in the richness which repays a second and a third reading. *Huckleberry Finn* can be taught profitably—though differently at different levels—all the way from junior high to graduate school; and many students will profit from more than one encounter with the book. It thus will serve as an ideal example to illustrate some differences in approach to novels for different levels. In the discussion which follows we will first consider some general problems in finding effective teaching strategies for presenting a book like *Huckleberry Finn* to students at different levels and then discuss the teaching of

---

1. Samuel L. Clemens, *The Adventures of Huckleberry Finn*, ed. by Lionel Trilling, Rinehart ed., no. 11 (New York: Rinehart and Company, Inc., 1948), pp. vi–vii.

Huckleberry Finn to junior high students, to senior high students, and to twelfth grade advanced placement students.

Arriving at teaching strategies

As he tries to arrive at effective teaching strategies for studying a given novel with any particular class, the teacher should ask two major questions: (1) How can I find the proper level of sophistication in my presentation of the novel so that my students' powers of understanding and their interests will be accommodated without distortion of the book itself? (2) How can I most usefully supplement in class what students will have gotten from the novel during their reading of it at home before class? The two questions are, to a degree, overlapping; but in answering the first, the teacher will wish to focus on the book itself, while in answering the second, he will want to focus on his students' reading habits and probable responses to the book.

As he focuses on the book itself with a view to determining his strategy for a particular class, the teacher should take account of three basic matters: *what* is told in the novel, *how* it is told, and *when* it was told. The *what* includes not only the series of events that happen, but the characters who are involved in them and the *point* or thematic implications of the story as well. The teacher must try to determine whether any points in the action will be unclear— either because it is hard to be sure what happens or because it is hard to understand the motivations for characters' actions. He should remember that at any level students will be interested in the *why* as well as the *what*—that they will want to discuss the motivation of the characters, not merely recount the events of the plot. Hence, the teacher should assess very carefully the degree to which any part of the motivation of the characters may be beyond his students' understanding. Understanding of theme comes from an understanding of event, character, and motivation, and with many books there is more than one thematic level, each dependent for its understanding upon an understanding of some aspect of motivation. Only as students are ready to understand increasingly complex motivations for characters' actions are they ready to understand increasingly sophisticated themes. Some themes in some books are out of the reach of the less sophisticated students; but there is no harm in presenting only the simpler thematic elements to these students, provided there is no distortion of the meaning of the book by suggesting motivations that are false. In other words, many books can be taught on different levels, as long as the teacher is careful to correlate the study of themes with the students' understanding of event and character.

In considering *how* the story is told the teacher should pay attention both to structure and to point of view. Structure involves questions both of chronology and of proportion; in most books it is not likely to be as important a consideration as point of view. Point of view, as was stated in Part Two, involves an understanding of the narrator and his attitudes. It is especially important for the teacher to try to foresee any confusion between author and narrator which may arise.

In taking account of *when* the story was told, the teacher simply decides how much background and footnoting to give. Are there things about the author and the time in which he wrote that are necessary to know in order to understand the book? In *Huckleberry Finn,* for example, the teacher will have to decide how much background about the nineteenth-century South and slavery he will wish to give the class, both to enable them to better understand the relationship between Jim and Huck—and hence part of the theme—and to prevent students from looking at racial questions in the book solely from the perspective of their own times and hence perhaps condemning it.

As the teacher asks the second major question—how he can best supplement and build in class on the understanding that students have already achieved—he may find it useful to consider the principle of "reverse teaching." This means, very simply, emphasizing in class those things which students cannot or do not achieve on their own and passing over more lightly those things which students have already discovered for themselves. In general, it would usually mean putting less emphasis on what happens (unless chronology is mixed up or events are ambiguous) and more on why it happens and what it means. But this principle will mean different things at different levels. In the case of those advanced students who may tend to jump to symbolic and thematic interpretations without paying enough attention to text, character, and event, it may mean stressing those things first. As John Knowles says, the story itself should always come first and then you can go on to the reverberations.[2]

A second answer to the second major question may be found in the generalization that students seldom get all that is to be found in a rich and complex text, and hence intensive study and discussion of significant portions of the text will supplement the vaguer, more

2. See p. 149.

fragmentary understanding and impressions students have acquired during their own reading. Such an approach will lead to a consideration of style in the broadest sense of that word. In the national survey of *High School English Instruction Today,* sponsored by the National Council of Teachers of English, the investigators found the need for more such teaching and described one successful example of it that they observed:

> Students have had a reading assignment, usually an entire work. They come to class with the book, and the teacher begins by asking a question about the text: "Here in this story by Dylan Thomas and in this one we have two opening sentences, the one about 40 words long, the other about 180 words long. How do you account for the difference?" After a number of comments that gradually range back and forth throughout other elements of each story, including symbols, details of characterization, and tone, it becomes apparent that the entire class discussion is devoted to the question of style in literature; and the students, at the end of the hour, have come to realize that style is a complex thing involving a great many elements besides the mere arrangement of words. It may well be that another teacher in the following year will also have something to say about style, but there will not be duplication of effort in the usual sense because the *discussion* is new: it will be on a higher, or at least different, level in [the] other class, and new elements will enter into it.[3]

Discussion of this sort focused on the text will help students to exchange insights and arrive at more complete understandings.

Finally, a third answer may be found in the simple injunction to remain as flexible as possible in responding to the questions that are of most interest to students or that trouble them most. It follows that the teacher will lecture very little—just enough to provide a bare minimum of background material or footnoting. It also follows that the teacher will not specify too rigid a plan for discussions—although he will have a strategy for raising issues of major importance, he will also be receptive to discussing issues which students raise. One investigator in the national survey mentioned above describes flexible classrooms of this sort in one outstanding school:

3. James R. Squire and Roger K. Applebee, *High School English Instruction Today* (New York: Appleton-Century-Crofts, 1968), p. 109.

The four teachers all said to their classes, in effect, "Look, we are all questioning the human condition. This book or play— *Macbeth, The Scarlet Letter, Lord of the Flies*—may tell us something about the human condition." These teachers expect their students to have adult motivations. There was no talking down and no phony talking up. They shared their students' wonder and helped each other eliminate their mutual ignorance. They looked at language and style and structure as well as theme and idea. The meaning of the book grew into something he had not seen before for everyone, teacher or student.[4]

And the authors agree that "this surely is the teaching of literature at its best."

A classroom of the general kind described is possible and desirable at any level. But, in considering any particular work, the teacher still needs to identify for himself, ahead of time, those particular things about "the human condition" or any other theme which that book will have to say most cogently to that particular class. Accordingly, in the section which follows we shall consider in some detail the kinds of insights that classes at the junior-high, senior-high, or twelfth-grade advanced placement levels might be led to achieve from a reading of *Huckleberry Finn*. At the same time we shall suggest some in-class activities which will usefully supplement the students' previous reading of the book at home.

Approaches for a junior-high class

At the junior-high level, perhaps the first understanding to achieve is that Huck, the narrator, is to be distinguished from Twain, the author. This distinction can be made at the beginning through a study of the text of the first chapter or part of it. Students then will not only begin to see that the way Huck tells his story helps to characterize him, but—more important—that his views and Twain's do not necessarily coincide. This will lay the necessary groundwork for understanding the two climactic scenes in which Huck decides not to turn Jim in. The first of these, in Chapter Sixteen, occurs just before Huck and Jim find out they have passed Cairo in the fog without knowing it. Huck has just managed to keep Jim from being discovered by pretending to a passing boat that it is his father with smallpox who is on the raft. His conscience bothers him but he realizes he would have felt equally bad if he had

4. *Ibid.*, p. 120.

given Jim up, and so he decides there's no use "learning to do right, when it's troublesome to do right and ain't no trouble to do wrong, and the wages is just the same."[5] The second passage, in Chapter Thirty-one, develops the same theme at greater length. Huck, his conscience still bothering him for not turning Jim in, tries to make excuses for himself because he "was brung up wicked," but then realizes that he is also responsible for his actions. "There was the Sunday-school," he tells himself, "you could 'a' gone to it; and if you'd 'a' done it they'd 'a' learnt you there that people that acts as I'd been acting about that nigger goes to everlasting fire." [Ch. XXXI, p. 270.] After a further struggle with his conscience while he debates whether to send a letter to Miss Watson telling her where Jim is, he finally tears up the letter and says, "All right, then, I'll *go* to hell." [Ch. XXXI, p. 272.] Students who have been trained earlier in the novel to keep Huck separate from Twain will be able to understand not only the courage with which Huck makes his decisions, but also Twain's condemnation of a society which uses its Sunday schools to teach that stealing of a slave is a sin, while slavery itself is not. Thus the book represents the process by which Huck—in spite of his society—comes to accept Jim as a human being.

In many junior-high classes, *Huckleberry Finn* may be taught as part of an English-Social Studies core curriculum. These classes will probably pay particular attention to the life along the river that Twain portrays, to the Grangerford-Shepherdson feud, to the question of slavery. At the same time, it is important that the book not become a mere case study for pre–Civil War American history and culture. One way to combat this problem is to keep the attention of the class focused on Huck and his reactions to what he sees and what happens to him, rather than on the events themselves. The teacher will ask how the feud has affected Huck, not just what happens in the feud. He will ask how Huck's attitudes toward slavery have been formed rather than merely asking what the society believes about slavery. A class that has started out making a clear distinction between Twain and Huck can be led to see each new series of incidents through Huck's eyes and to discuss finally the questions: Does Huck grow up? Is he changed by the events of the book?

Even at the junior-high level, students should begin to make critical judgments, not about good and bad books so much as about better or worse ones. This implies the development of comparison

5. Samuel L. Clemens, *The Adventures of Huckleberry Finn* (New York: Charles L. Webster and Company, 1885), Ch. XVI, p. 128. Subsequent quotations are taken from this first edition.

and contrast as a major critical tool, perhaps through an extended comparison with another book that students have read recently. Twain's own *Tom Sawyer* would serve well, both because it has many of the same characters and because at its center there is the parallel episode in which Tom, Joe Harper, and Huck Finn run away to Jackson's Island to play at being pirates. If students compare the two books—especially Chapters Eight to Eleven of *Huckleberry Finn* with Chapters Thirteen to Sixteen of *Tom Sawyer*—they will find many parallels: the steamboat searching for a dead body, firing its cannon, and dispersing loaves of bread with quicksilver in them; a stealthy visit to the shore to spy on the townspeople and ascertain their plans; a severe thunderstorm and some description of nature; discussion of superstitions, of loneliness, of conscience.

But in spite of these similarities, the effect of each book is quite different, partly because the issues raised in *Huckleberry Finn* are of a very different magnitude from those in *Tom Sawyer*, partly because the use of Huck as narrator provides a more skillful and satisfactory technique than Twain's use of the omniscient author-narrator in *Tom Sawyer*. Students who can be brought to these two realizations will have begun to make important judgments about quality.

The difference in magnitude between the issues in the two books may be appreciated by pointing to two contrasts. The teacher can use selected passages to lead students to see the first contrast between playing at something and being involved in the more serious business of survival. In *Tom Sawyer*, even though the disappearance of the boys is serious business for their families, the boys themselves are simply pleased with "their new grandeur and the illustrious trouble they were making."[6] When he goes ashore to spy on his family in Chapter Fifteen, Tom resists the impulse to disclose himself even when he hears his Aunt Polly's grief while he is hiding under the bed. And we are invited to share Tom's perspective rather than his aunt's, to think of the prank of attending his own funeral as worth the heartache to his family. The game is the important thing, not the reality. Huck and Jim, on the other hand, run the real risk of capture and are playing for considerably higher stakes. They feel no need, as Tom does, to avoid the "comfortable path along the shore . . . [because] it lacked the advantages of difficulty and danger so valued by a pirate." [*Tom Sawyer*, Ch. XIII, p. 115.] They have real difficulties enough without playing at increasing them. Students might be led to see this contrast between

6. Samuel L. Clemens, *The Adventures of Tom Sawyer* (San Francisco: American Publishing Company, 1876), Ch. XIV, p. 126. Subsequent quotations are taken from this first edition.

the two books if they were asked questions like these: What would the boys do differently in *Tom Sawyer* if they were not playing a game? Why do the boys in *Tom Sawyer* get lonesome and home-sick so soon? And how does Huck in *Huckleberry Finn* avoid get-ting lonesome? The following passage from *Huckleberry Finn* might be useful in answering the last question:

> When it was dark I set by my camp fire smoking, and feeling pretty satisfied; but by-and-by it got sort of lonesome, and so I went and set on the bank and listened to the currents washing along, and counted the stars and drift-logs and rafts that come down, and then went to bed; there ain't no better way to put in time when you are lonesome; you can't stay so, you soon get over it. [Ch. VIII, p. 64.]

Huck is beginning to achieve a kind of harmony with nature that the boys in *Tom Sawyer,* knowing that they can always go home, do not. In *Huckleberry Finn* the stakes are greater and involve the shaping of a whole new life.

The second contrast in the situations of the two books involves the nature of the dangers the characters face. There are indeed times in *Tom Sawyer* when the issues are literally life and death ones, but these occasions are different from analogous ones in *Huckleberry Finn* because in the earlier book the struggle is between individuals and does not involve any social dimension; Injun Joe is a threat because he is a villain, not because he represents society in any way. Pap Finn is the same kind of threat in the later book, but we soon move away from that kind of threat to the threats posed by the many kinds of social corruption that Huck encounters, rang-ing all the way from the feud, to the chicanery of the Duke and the King, to the corruption of slavery itself that has already been dis-cussed. This social dimension also raises the magnitude of the is-sues in the book, and students can be led to see this contrast between the two books by such questions as these: What is exciting in *Tom Sawyer?* In *Huckleberry Finn?* What is the difference in the dangers that provide some of the excitement in the two books? Responses to these questions will probably enable the teacher to move into a discussion of the ways in which society poses obstacles and dangers to Huck and Jim.

The fact that Huck is narrator in the later book helps to in-crease the sense of excitement and intensify the conflicts between Huck and society—but it does more than this. It gives a sense of immediacy, credibility, and realism to the later book that the earlier one lacks. Just as the boys in *Tom Sawyer* play games with each other, so Twain plays games with them as he tells his story. He looks down on them in condescending, though amused fashion as he describes the incident in which Tom and Joe get sick while learning to smoke:

Now they stretched themselves out on their elbows and began to puff, charily, and with slender confidence. The smoke had an unpleasant taste, and they gagged a little, but Tom said:

"Why it's just as easy! If I'd a knowed *this* was all, I'd a learnt long ago."

"So would I," said Joe. "It's just nothing."

"Why many a time I've looked at people smoking, and thought well I wish I could do that; but I never thought I could," said Tom.

"That's just the way with me, hain't it Huck? You've heard me talk just that way—haven't you Huck? I'll leave it to Huck if I haven't."

"Yes—heaps of times," said Huck.

"Well I have too," said Tom; "O, hundreds of times. Once down by the slaughter-house. Don't you remember, Huck? Bob Tanner was there, and Johnny Miller, and Jeff Thatcher, when I said it. Don't you remember Huck, 'bout me saying that?"

"Yes, that's so," said Huck. "That was the day after I lost a white alley. No, 'twas the day before."

"There—I told you so," said Tom. "Huck recollects it."

"I bleeve I could smoke this pipe all day," said Joe. "*I* don't feel sick."

"Neither do I," said Tom. "*I* could smoke it all day. But I bet you Jeff Thatcher couldn't."

"Jeff Thatcher! Why he'd keel over just with two draws. Just let him try it once. *He'd* see!"

"I bet he would. And Johnny Miller—I wish I could see Johnny Miller tackle it once."

"O, don't *I!*" said Joe, "Why I bet you Johnny Miller couldn't any more do this than nothing. Just one little snifter would fetch *him.*"

"'Deed it would, Joe. Say—I wish the boys could see us now."

"So do I."

"Say—boys, don't say anything about it, and some time when they're around, I'll come up to you and say 'Joe, got a pipe? I want a smoke.' And you'll say, kind of careless like, as if it warn't anything, you'll say, 'Yes, I got my *old* pipe, and another one, but my tobacker ain't very good.' And I'll say, 'Oh, that's all right, if it's *strong* enough.' And then you'll out with the pipes, and we'll light up just as ca'm, and then just see 'em look!"

"By jings that'll be gay, Tom! I wish it was *now!*"

"So do I! And when we tell 'em we learned when we was off pirating, won't they wish they'd been along?"

"O, I reckon not! I'll just *bet* they will!"

So the talk ran on. But presently it began to flag a trifle, and grow disjointed. The silences widened; the expectoration marvelously increased. Every pore inside the boys' cheeks became a spouting fountain; they could scarcely bail out the cellars under their tongues fast enough to prevent an inundation; little overflowings down their throats occurred in spite of all they could do, and sudden retchings followed every time. Both boys were looking very pale and miserable, now. Joe's pipe dropped from his nerveless fingers. Tom's followed. Both fountains were going furiously and both pumps bailing with might and main. Joe said feebly:

"I've lost my knife. I reckon I better go and find it."

Tom said, with quivering lips and halting utterance:

"I'll help you. You go over that way and I'll hunt around by the spring. No, you needn't come, Huck—we can find it."

So Huck sat down again, and waited an hour. Then he found it lonesome, and went to find his comrades. They were wide apart in the woods, both very pale, both fast asleep. But something informed him that if they had had any trouble they had got rid of it.

They were not talkative at supper that night. They had a humble look, and when Huck prepared his pipe after the meal and was going to prepare theirs, they said no, they were not feeling very well—something they ate at dinner had disagreed with them. [Ch. XVI, pp. 138–140.]

Later he leaves them "to smoke and chatter and brag, since we have no further use for them at present." [Ch. XVI, p. 143.] In *Huckleberry Finn,* in contrast, though we are constantly aware of Huck as the narrator, we never have the sense that he is manipulating people or events in telling his story. He is not playing the game of author: he is simply telling what happened to him.

One can see the difference between Twain as narrator in *Tom Sawyer* and Huck as narrator in *Huckleberry Finn* even in the description of similar incidents. Compare Twain's description of the storm with Huck's description of a similar storm which he and Jim watch from their cave:

> About midnight Joe awoke, and called the boys. There was a brooding oppressiveness in the air that seemed to bode something. The boys huddled themselves together and sought the friendly companionship of the fire, though the dull dead heat of the breathless atmosphere was stifling. They sat still, intent and waiting. The solemn hush continued. Beyond the light of the fire everything was swallowed up in the blackness of darkness. Presently there came a quivering glow that vaguely revealed the foliage for a moment and then vanished. By and by another came, a little stronger. Then another. Then a faint moan came sighing through the branches of the forest and the boys felt a fleeting breath upon their cheeks, and shuddered with the fancy that the Spirit of the Night had gone by. There was a pause. Now a weird flash turned night into day and showed every little grass-blade, separate and distinct, that grew about their feet. And it showed three white, startled faces, too. A deep peal of thunder went rolling and tumbling down the heavens and lost itself in sullen rumblings in the distance. A sweep of chilly air passed by, rustling all the leaves and snowing the flaky ashes broadcast about the fire. Another fierce glare lit up the forest and an instant crash followed that seemed to rend the tree-tops right over the boys' heads. They clung together in terror, in the thick gloom that followed. A few big raindrops fell pattering upon the leaves.
>
> "Quick! boys, go for the tent!" exclaimed Tom.
>
> They sprang away, stumbling over roots and among vines in the dark, no two plunging in the same direction. A furious blast roared through the trees, making everything sing as it went. One blinding flash after another came, and peal on peal of deafening thunder. And now a drenching rain poured down and the rising hurricane drove it in sheets along the ground. The boys cried out to each other, but the roaring wind and the booming thunder-blasts drowned their voices utterly. However one by one they straggled in at last and took shelter under the tent, cold, scared, and streaming with water; but to have company in misery seemed something to be grateful for. They could not talk, the old sail flapped so furiously, even if the other noises would have allowed them. The tempest rose higher and higher, and presently the sail tore loose from its fastenings and went winging away on the blast. The boys seized each other's hands and fled, with many tumblings and

bruises, to the shelter of a great oak that stood upon the river bank. Now the battle was at its highest. Under the ceaseless conflagration of lightning that flamed in the skies, everything below stood out in clean-cut and shadowless distinctness: the bending trees, the billowy river, white with foam, the driving spray of spume-flakes, the dim outlines of the high bluffs on the other side, glimpsed through the drifting cloud-rack and the slanting veil of rain. Every little while some giant tree yielded the fight and fell crashing through the younger growth; and the unflagging thunder-peals came now in ear-splitting explosive bursts, keen and sharp, and unspeakably appalling. The storm culminated in one matchless effort that seemed likely to tear the island to pieces, burn it up, drown it to the tree tops, blow it away, and deafen every creature in it, all at one and the same moment. It was a wild night for homeless young heads to be out in. [*Tom Sawyer,* Ch. XVI, pp. 140–142.]

Pretty soon it darkened up and begun to thunder and lighten; so the birds was right about it. Directly it begun to rain, and it rained like all fury, too, and I never see the wind blow so. It was one of these regular summer storms. It would get so dark that it looked all blue-black outside, and lovely; and the rain would thrash along by so thick that the trees off a little ways looked dim and spider-webby; and here would come a blast of wind that would bend the trees down and turn up the pale underside of the leaves; and then a perfect ripper of a gust would follow along and set the branches to tossing their arms as if they was just wild; and next, when it was just about the bluest and blackest—*fst!* it was as bright as glory and you'd have a little glimpse of tree-tops a-plunging about, away off yonder in the storm, hundreds of yards further than you could see before; dark as sin again in a second, and now you'd hear the thunder let go with an awful crash and then go rumbling, grumbling, tumbling, down the sky towards the under side of the world, like rolling empty barrels down stairs, where it's long stairs and they bounce a good deal, you know.

"Jim, this is nice," I says. "I wouldn't want to be nowhere else but here. Pass me along another hunk of fish and some hot corn-bread." [*Huckleberry Finn,* Ch. IX, pp. 75–76.]

In the passage from *Tom Sawyer* we look down at the scene from a vantage point and see the boys and the storm—and we see parts of the scene that they cannot see, for our view is panoramic. In *Huckleberry Finn,* we look through Huck's eyes at the storm and we share his thoughts as he sees it. His description is fully as rich as Twain's in *Tom Sawyer,* but the descriptive technique, reflected in both word and metaphor, is entirely appropriate to Huck's character. The description in the earlier book comes dangerously close to being a detachable set piece; the description in *Huckleberry Finn* blends nicely into its surroundings in the book.

A similar contrast can be seen between this passage in the earlier book and Huck's description in the later book:

> They lay around in the shade, after breakfast, while Huck had a smoke, and then went off through the woods on an exploring expedition. They tramped gaily along, over decaying logs, through tangled underbrush, among solemn monarchs of the forest, hung from their crowns to the ground with a drooping regalia of grape-vines. Now and then they came upon snug nooks carpeted with grass and jeweled with flowers. [*Tom Sawyer,* Ch. XIV, p. 123.]

> The sun was up so high when I waked, that I judged it was after eight o'clock. I laid there in the grass and the cool shade, thinking about things and feeling rested and ruther comfortable and satisfied. I could see the sun out at one or two holes, but mostly it was big trees all about, and gloomy in there amongst them. There was freckled places on the ground where the light sifted down through the leaves, and the freckled places swapped about a little, showing there was a little breeze up there. A couple of squirrels set on a limb and jabbered at me very friendly. [*Huckleberry Finn,* Ch. VIII, p. 61.]

Huck describes the scene as he sees it . . . and in a way which will seem much more natural to adolescent as well as to adult readers.

Approaches for an eleventh-grade class

Some of these same contrasts between the two books could also be profitably made by an eleventh-grade class. At this level discussion might center around the major questions: What does the use of Huck as narrator allow Twain to do in *Huckleberry Finn* that he can't do in *Tom Sawyer?* What is the difference between the two narrators? Which point of view has the greater advantage for telling the story of

Huckleberry Finn? Both narrators are intrusive, since both comment on the story they are telling, though, as I have pointed out above, we find that some of Twain's comments in *Tom Sawyer* take away from the realism of the book by suggesting too strongly the manipulations of the author.

Huck, in contrast, has a more limited view of things, but this very limitation is useful in making us see events through his eyes. And Huck's intrusions are of a different sort from Twain's, for Huck is a thoroughly naive narrator, Twain an authoritative one. The naive narrator serves an irreplaceable function in *Huckleberry Finn:* the evils in Twain's society come into sharper focus as we see them through Huck's eyes because—ironically—Huck usually accepts as a matter of course that society must be right and his own natural instincts and inclinations wrong. This irony is at the heart of the theme of the book and could not be so effectively worked out if an omniscient author-narrator were telling the story.

An eleventh-grade class should be able to explore the ironies in *Huckleberry Finn* in some depth. They lie in the continuing contrast between life on the raft and life on the shore and in the contrast between Huck's perceptions and values and the perceptions and values of society.

The contrast between raft and shore is a continuing one. On the raft days and nights "swum by, they slid along so quiet and smooth and lovely." Compared to a raft, other places "seem so cramped up and smothery," Huck says, for "You feel mighty free and easy and comfortable on a raft." [*Huckleberry Finn,* Ch. XIX, p. 157; Ch. XVIII, p. 156.][7] "[W]e was always naked, day and night, whenever the mosquitoes would let us," Huck says [Ch. XIX, p. 159.], and it is not surprising that he and Jim should feel more "comfortable" without clothes, the symbols not only of discomfort but of the hypocrisy of society, where clothes are one more manifestation of the difference between surface and essence or appearance and reality, as well as being a barrier between man and nature. On the raft Huck is at ease and happy, though he is not necessarily a better person, as is shown by the incident in which Huck serves Jim a mean trick and tries to convince him he has dreamt what has actually happened. Even here, however, the raft makes a difference, for here Jim can speak out against Huck:

"When I got all wore out wid work, en wid de callin' for you, en went to sleep, my heart wuz mos' broke bekase you wuz los', en I

---

7. Cf. *Huckleberry Finn,* Ch. XIX, p. 166: "[W]hat you want, above all things, on a raft, is for everybody to be satisfied, and feel right and kind towards the others."

didn' k'yer no mo' what become er me en de raf'. En when I wake up en fine you back agin', all safe en soun', de tears come en I could a got down on my knees en kiss' yo' foot I's so thankful. En all you wuz thinkin 'bout wuz how you could make a fool uv ole Jim wid a lie." [Ch. XV, p. 121.]

And it is easier for Huck to ask Jim's forgiveness than it would be on shore:

> It was fifteen minutes before I could work myself up to go and humble myself to a nigger—but I done it, and I warn't ever sorry for it afterwards, neither. [Ch. XV, p. 121.]

Life on the shore, even at its best, cannot approach life on the raft. And at its worst there are the feud with its cruelty disguised under the name of honor, the shooting down of the drunken Boggs in undisguised cold blood by Colonel Sherburn, and the schemes of those two con men par excellence, the King and the Duke. And the con men succeed in part because the people they cheat deserve no better fate than to be cheated:

> The hogs loafed and grunted around, everywheres. You'd see a muddy sow and a litter of pigs come lazying along the street and whollop herself right down in the way, where folks had to walk around her, and she'd stretch out, and shut her eyes, and wave her ears, whilst the pigs was milking her, and look as happy as if she was on salary. And pretty soon you'd hear a loafer sing out, "Hi! *so* boy! sick him, Tige!" and away the sow would go, squealing most horrible, with a dog or two swinging to each ear, and three or four dozen more a-coming; and then you would see all the loafers get up and watch the thing out of sight, and laugh at the fun and look grateful for the noise. Then they'd settle back again till there was a dog-fight. There couldn't anything wake them up all over, and make them happy all over, like a dog-fight—unless it might be putting turpentine on a stray dog and setting fire to him, or tying a tin pan to his tail and see him run himself to death. [Ch. XXI, p. 183.]

But even when the King and the Duke get the fate they deserve, Huck, whose instincts for kindness lie deep within him and are identified with the life on the raft, pities them and regrets their being tarred and feathered:

> Well, it made me sick to see it; and I was sorry for them poor

pitiful rascals, it seemed like I couldn't ever feel any hardness against them any more in the world. It was a dreadful thing to see. Human beings *can* be awful cruel to one another. [Ch. XXXIII, p. 291.]

Huck's sympathy for the King and the Duke, though stemming in part from the kindness of his nature, comes in part from another source as well—and thus represents a greater complexity in his character than might at first appear. For in spite of the trouble they cause Huck and Jim, Huck has a sneaking admiration for the King and the Duke. Perhaps he sees in them something of the shrewdness he has had to develop himself in order to survive. "Them rapscallions took in four hundred and sixty-five dollars in that three nights," Huck says. "I never see money hauled in by the wagon-load like that, before." [Ch. XXIII, p. 199.] And a little later, as he watches them try to take in the Wilks girls, he says, "If they warn't the beatenest lot, them two frauds, that ever I struck." But his feelings are ambiguous, for three sentences later he is saying, "It was enough to make a body ashamed of the human race." [Ch. XXIV, p. 210.] A bit later he resolves to protect Mary Jane from their schemes, and after their treachery to Jim, he loses any trace of admiration (though, as noted above, he will finally express pity for them):

After all this long journey, and after all we'd done for them scoundrels, here was it all come to nothing, everything all busted up and ruined, because they could have the heart to serve Jim such a trick as that, and make him a slave again all his life, and amongst strangers, too, for forty dirty dollars. [Ch. XXXI, p. 269.]

Huck, then, is more than just the naive narrator or the innocent natural man. He is also the shrewd frontiersman, not to mention the boy growing up and receiving his initiation into the complexities and the evils of the adult world. He is neither thoroughly naive (though he sometimes appears so in his acceptance of the values of society when they conflict with his natural instincts and inclinations), nor thoroughly sophisticated (though his system of values and his conduct are much more rational than those of the society around him). In short, in his character Twain has underscored the major irony of the book: the contrast between the natural world and the social world and the contradiction between the ideals the social world professes and the perversion and negation of those ideals in practice. Eleventh-graders can be brought to insights of the sort discussed above through questions which focus on the ironies in situation and character and on the use of Huck as narrator.

Similar perspectives might also be gained by comparing the ending of the book with the endings of Hugo Butler's screenplay and John Seelye's retelling of *Huckleberry Finn.* In the course of comparing the three endings, students should both deal with the problem that Twain's ending has raised for many critics and see how the use of Huck as narrator helps to make the effect of the book different from that of the movie. (For excerpts from the screenplay and the Seelye version, see the Appendix.)

Perhaps the main difference between the motion picture script and the book is the greater emphasis in the former on action and suspense. The alternating cuts of Jim's trial, incarceration, and near-lynching with Huck's sickbed, delirium, and frantic attempts to reach Jim in time, provide the kind of visual excitement and suspense that the motion picture form finds congenial. But the ironies in the contrasts between raft and shore and in the discrepancies between Huck's natural impulses and society's values begin to disappear, for Huck as naive narrator is necessary to bring those out. On the other hand, the focus of the action in the screenplay is kept more firmly on Huck (who is the one wounded by the rattlesnake, in contrast to Tom's gunshot wound in the book) and Jim (who, as in the book, gives up his freedom to help a white man but is placed in more immediate danger). At the very end of the film-script Huck has agreed to the Widow's terms of going to school, wearing shoes, and giving up smoking—even though in our last glimpse of him he is barefoot and there is a pipe in his pocket. The implication is that he has made a bargain which he will try to keep, though perhaps unsuccessfully, and that that bargain is a relatively desirable one. The end of the book, in contrast, implies that Huck has not come to terms with "civilization": "But I reckon I got to light out for the Territory ahead of the rest, because Aunt Sally she's going to adopt me and sivilize me and I can't stand it. I been there before." [Ch. the last, p. 366.] Our reading of the rest of the book will suggest that Huck is rejecting "civilization" not only because it means uncomfortable clothes, long hours in school, and other nuisances, but also because it has shown itself to bad advantage in whatever experiences he has had, whether with the feud, with the Duke and the King, or with the general stupidity and cruelty of the inhabitants of the shore. The ending of the screenplay does not suggest this rejection.

John Seelye's retelling of the story, on the other hand, focuses even more sharply than Twain does on Huck's rejection of society and the shore. Indeed, Huck's experience with society in this version, in which Jim comes to a tragic end, so embitters him that the revision ends on a note of nihilistic despair. Although the ironies and the contrasts between river and shore and between nature and civilization are maintained, they are subordinated to the overall tragic effect of the final section. An eleventh-grade class should be able to see that Seelye has left the ironies intact—Huck still struggles with his conscience and attributes to the workings of "Providence" things that should be attributed to the corruption of society—even though they may not be able to fully appreciate the ways in which tone and mood have been changed.

Approaches for a twelfth-grade advanced placement class

Seelye's rewriting is, of course, in response to those many critics who have found the ending of the book to be weaker than the rest of it. And a twelfth-grade advanced placement class might deal very specifically with that problem. The charges against the ending are that it is anticlimactic, that Twain somehow falls below his previous level in the book and succumbs to his tendency to low comedy, and that Jim is treated cruelly, thus threatening the previous development of both character and theme. In assessing these charges, students should consider alternatives to the ending, among them those of the screenplay and Seelye's version. In the book, the Widow's freeing of Jim is a kind of *deus ex machina,* since we have not been prepared for her change of heart. In the script, Huck appears to win Jim's freedom by his bargain with the Widow, though we are probably not meant to think that the bargain will be kept very rigidly. In the script Huck also saves Jim's life by leaving his sickbed and arriving at the jail in the nick of time, providing a certain fitness in the rescue. The rescue of Jim in the book, engineered by Tom in a parody of the best romantic tradition, tends to throw Huck into the shade as a character and hence, some critics charge, to negate previous development of character and theme. The script may thus seem to solve some of the problems posed by the ending of the book, although it creates others of its own in a tendency toward melodrama and less complexity of theme and character.

Seelye's version, in contrast, maintains the complexity of theme and character, though it raises other questions. Chief among these is the question whether a tragic ending is logically and tonally in keeping with the rest of the book. A twelfth-grade advanced placement class might deal with this question, considering whether Jim's fate results inevitably from the situations and the antebellum society described, or whether this fate is, in a curious way, analogous to the melodrama of the screenplay, serving mainly a propagandistic purpose in arousing our feelings against slavery. A further question—whether the hopelessness and despair of the revised ending is in keeping with the satire and humor of the rest of the book—is likewise worthy of consideration.

Finally, the question arises whether either the ending of the screenplay or the ending of Seelye's version is clearly superior in every way to Twain's ending. Thorough discussion of this question should lead students, not to a single answer, but to increased understanding of all three versions. Discussion should also lead them to see that Twain's ending has virtues which may not at first appear, for the fact that Huck reacts to Tom's plans in the same way he has reacted to society's codes earlier in the book—he assumes that his own common sense plan is inferior—helps to maintain a consistent irony. And Twain's ending also makes a final thrust at society, as telling in its way as Seelye's: for the ridiculous child's plan, even though it is modeled on adult romanticism, succeeds against the adult world because that world has made itself vulnerable through its own ridiculousness. There is a kind of cathartic effect from the outwitting of the adults. The freeing of Jim also serves another psychological function for the reader: it softens the effect of the *deus ex machina* of the Widow's will, which might otherwise seem even less satisfactory to us. And that *deus ex machina* itself provides a final irony: in the antebellum South it is appropriate that Jim's freedom should depend on a seemingly whimsical change of heart; to suggest that he could achieve it through his own efforts would have been less realistic and might have tended toward the kind of melodrama that occurs in the script. Finally, though Jim's story can be resolved with finality with his freedom, Huck's fate is less susceptible to a final outcome; and the final two sentences of the book are a more appropriate conclusion than the seemingly more definite conclusion of the script. The note of resilience may also appear to be more in keeping with the rest of the book than the despair of Seelye's version. An advanced placement class should profit from debating some of the strengths and weaknesses of Twain's ending, keeping the motion picture script and Seelye's revision as points of reference and comparison.

But a class would be ready to discuss the ending only after prolonged discussion of other important aspects of Twain's book. An advanced class could profit especially from a consideration of the theme of freedom and bondage and the related theme of conscience. Here again, an irony is central: Jim, though a slave, is in some ways freer than Huck, who has to fight to free himself from the social conditioning that has produced slavery, literal and figurative, as well as other social corruptions. It is interesting that in the last part of the book Jim's freedom is never seriously in doubt. When he is imprisoned on the Phelps plantation, Tom and Huck agree that they can free him quickly in any emergency and they even have to free Jim momentarily so that he can help them bring the grindstone back to the cabin. Jim, as noted above, is free—especially on the raft—to respond to Huck as another human being, and he berates Huck for trying to fool him. Huck, while on the raft, is also relatively free to respond naturally to Jim and he does ask his pardon. But Huck finds it harder to free himself of society. Even when he says, "All right, then, I'll *go* to hell," Huck is still thinking in society's terms. For "conscience" is the creation of society: it is conscience that makes Huck uneasy in aiding Jim to escape and conscience that makes him generally uncomfortable—uncomfortable even when the King and the Duke, who have harmed him and Jim and for whose fate he is not responsible, are tarred and feathered:

> So we poked along back home, and I warn't feeling so brash as I was before, but kind of ornery, and humble, and to blame, somehow—though *I* hadn't done nothing. But that's always the way; it don't make no difference whether you do right or wrong, a person's conscience ain't got no sense, and just goes for him *anyway*. If I had a yaller dog that didn't know no more than a person's conscience does, I would pison him. It takes up more room than all the rest of a person's insides, and yet ain't no good, nohow. Tom Sawyer he says the same. [Ch. XXXIII, pp. 291–292.]

Though Tom may "say the same," his attitude is somewhat different from Huck's, because he has accepted society's adult world more thoroughly than Huck has. Whereas Huck's conscience makes him feel uneasy at diverging from society's commands in helping Jim, Tom, it is made clear, would not have helped to free Jim if he hadn't known that Jim was already free. And the plan he has for doing it is in some ways a boy's version of the same kind of romantic and elaborate, yet cruel and senseless code that we have seen in the feud. In spite of its disadvantages, Twain's ending in some ways reinforces the indictment of society he has made in the rest of the book.

An advanced placement class might also be led to see that indictment partly through the symbolic dimension of the book, perhaps comparing the raft with Thoreau's cabin if they have previously read *Walden*. Just as Thoreau's cabin is an oasis surrounded by "the mass of men" leading "lives of quiet desperation,"[8] the raft is an

---

8. Henry D. Thoreau, "Economy," *Walden; or, Life in the Woods* (Garden City, N.Y.: Dolphin Books, Doubleday and Company, Inc., n.d.), p. 11. Reprint of 1st edition of 1854.

oasis surrounded by the corrupt life of the shore. Thoreau went to Walden because he wished "to front only the essential facts of life . . . to drive life into a corner, and reduce it to its lowest terms."[9] Though Huck is forced into his situation rather than choosing it, the experience of life on the raft is very much like that of life in the cabin. And as each oasis provides the opportunity to front life's essentials, the ways in which man is slave to society are revealed. Thoreau says:

> I sometimes wonder that we can be so frivolous, I may almost say, as to attend to the gross but somewhat foreign form of servitude called Negro Slavery, there are so many keen and subtle masters that enslave both north and south. It is hard to have a southern overseer; it is worse to have a northern one; but worst of all when you are the slave-driver of yourself. Talk of a divinity in man! Look at the teamster on the highway, wending to market by day or night; does any divinity stir within him? His highest duty to fodder and water his horses! What is his destiny to him compared with the shipping interests? Does not he drive for Squire Make-a-stir? How godlike, how immortal, is he? See how he cowers and sneaks, how vaguely all the day he fears, not being immortal nor divine, but the slave and prisoner of his own opinion of himself, a fame won by his own deeds. Public opinion is a weak tyrant compared with our own private opinion. What a man thinks of himself, that it is which determines, or rather indicates, his fate.[10]

Until his climactic decision to "go to hell," Huck is the "slave and prisoner of his own opinion of himself,"—and, in Twain's terms, of his conscience—and this is a kind of slavery from which Jim is exempt. Huck can finally throw off this slavery (and then not completely or permanently) only because the raft in its isolation provides an opportunity to front the essential facts of life. In Thoreau's terms, Huck finally discovers and obeys "the laws of his being,"[11] even though those laws conflict with society's. Like the cabin in *Walden,* the raft in *Huck Finn* is a symbolic center of the book.

Finally, an advanced placement class might consider Twain's style on a fairly sophisticated level. Take, for example, this passage describing the undertaker at Peter Wilks' funeral:

9. *Ibid.,* "Where I Lived and What I Lived For," p. 80.
10. *Ibid.,* "Economy," pp. 10–11.
11. *Ibid.,* "Conclusion," p. 271.

When the place was packed full, the undertaker he slid around in his black gloves with his softy soothering ways, putting on the last touches, and getting people and things all ship-shape and comfortable, and making no more sound than a cat. He never spoke; he moved people around, he squeezed in late ones, he opened up passage-ways, and done it all with nods, and signs with his hands. Then he took his place over against the wall. He was the softest, glidingest, stealthiest man I ever see; and there warn't no more smile to him than there is to a ham. [Ch. XXVII, p. 232.]

This comic vignette is a masterpiece in economy and suggestion, for it not only suggests the character of the undertaker but also gives an equally skillful revelation of Huck, the narrator. The passage will repay a careful look at language, tone, and detail, with attention paid to such words as "soothering" and "glidingest" (Huck's invention), to such details as the gloves and the nods and signs, and to the two metaphors—"no more sound than a cat" and "no more smile . . . than . . . a ham." *Huckleberry Finn* abounds in similarly rich passages for stylistic consideration.

Summary

Any attempt to summarize the teaching strategies which have been suggested is likely to oversimplify; but it might be useful to review the major strategies, keeping in mind the two major questions about the proper level of sophistication and the best way to supplement in class what students have learned on their own outside of class:

1. At the junior-high level, the first insight to convey to students is that Twain, the author, and Huck, the narrator, are not one and the same. Students at this level may not be ready to consider all the ramifications of making Huck the narrator, but they should be ready to trace his relationship with Jim and to understand something of the backdrop against which that relationship is developed. They should also be able to sense at least part of the indictment of slavery and other social ills, keeping their focus on Huck's reaction to what he sees. Finally, they should be able to make some comparisons with other books—perhaps with *Tom Sawyer*—and to assess some of the special strengths of *Huckleberry Finn*. These insights should be within the grasp of most junior-high students. The insights students will be least likely to develop outside of class will be those that come from

comparison with other books—this is one activity that the teacher can arrange which is not apt to take place otherwise.

2. At the senior-high level a class should be able to make meaningful contrasts with other books—perhaps again with *Tom Sawyer*—and to understand more fully the results of having Huck as narrator. They should be able to consider point of view in a somewhat more sophisticated fashion, speculating about alternatives and ramifications. They should also appreciate the central ironies of the book: the contrasts between raft and shore, the discrepancy between Huck's impulses and society's values with the tendency of Huck to deprecate his own feelings and believe that society is right. They should be able to appreciate some of the complexity and ambivalence of Huck's character. Finally, they should be able to discuss the ending of the book intelligently, considering its strengths and weaknesses and the possible alternatives—among them the motion picture script and Seelye's version—in relation to the insights discussed above. Here, as with the junior-high class, the teacher can increase in-class insights by setting up comparisons that would not have occurred or been available to students on their own.

3. A senior-high advanced placement class may need first of all to be led to appreciate the story as a story, for in their own reading they may jump too quickly to the symbolic level. On the level of symbol and theme, they should be able to discuss the ending with a good deal of sophistication, drawing upon their understanding of the complex themes such as freedom and bondage in the rest of the book to judge the strengths and weaknesses of the ending. They may also find it profitable to make comparisons with other books they have read, such as Thoreau's *Walden,* in that case comparing the symbolic importance of cabin and raft. Finally, they should be able to undertake a fairly sophisticated stylistic analysis of selected passages of the book.

Among the many worlds of *Huckleberry Finn* there may not be one for literally every reader to explore; but the possibilities are rich, and the teacher who is prepared to be flexible in his presentation of the book will find that many different kinds of classes can profit from it.

PART FOUR

Approaching Novels

A Unit on the Black Experience

A famous teacher once suggested that a good answer to the question "How can you best fit boys and girls for the life of men and women?" was to get them "out of the ruts of custom—by confronting them with things unfamiliar, things rather troublesome, things that require mental . . . exertion." He admitted that this might "make havoc with a great many cherished ideas, maxims, schemes," and raise the question "whether very new literature is good teaching matter."

Another famous teacher had expressed this same major idea a few years before, suggesting that the greatest danger to true education comes from "inert ideas," that is, "ideas that are merely received into the mind without being utilised, or tested, or thrown into fresh combinations." The "central problem of all education," he believed, is "the problem of keeping knowledge alive, of preventing it from becoming inert." And one way to do this is to lead students to "experience the joy of discovery" as they strive to understand the world around them.

It was George Saintsbury[1] and Alfred North Whitehead[2] who made these statements, and they made them more than fifty years

---

1. George Saintsbury, "On the Teaching of English," *The Athenaeum* (July 9, 1920); reprinted in *George Saintsbury; The Memorial Volume; A New Collection of His Essays and Papers,* 2nd ed., (London: Methuen & Company, Ltd., 1946), pp. 191–193.
2. Alfred North Whitehead, *The Aims of Education and Other Essays* (New York: The Macmillan Company, 1929), pp. 1–7.

ago; but the issues are as vital as ever today. Students must be brought "out of the ruts of custom," and must be confronted, not with "inert ideas," but with knowledge that is "alive" and "things unfamiliar." The task is not an easy one, but literature—and especially "new literature"—can achieve this result in a way that nothing else can, for if well chosen and well taught, it engages both the minds and the emotions of students.

We have heard increasingly in the last few years talk of "relevance," in such various contexts as the Dartmouth Seminar, speeches by leaders in the profession, and the demands of students themselves. But the definitions of relevance have not always been clear. Does it mean simply using contemporary materials? Does it mean using materials geared to the ability or interests of students? Does it mean using materials that treat controversial social issues? Or does it have more to do with the way that materials are used than with the materials themselves? Does it perhaps mean guiding a class to see some of the things that a popular song and a poem may share or the ways in which Chaucer's pilgrims are kin to such pilgrims as the peace marchers on Washington? The answer to these questions lies, I think, in the fact that relevance cannot be narrowly defined as a single thing: it means both discovering the universal and the unusual in the familiar and enlarging the student's horizons and stretching his mind through an understanding of the remote. We have not always realized that, paradoxically, things that are ultimately most "relevant" to the development of students may well be furthest from their immediate experience. And conversely, things that are closest to them must often be given a certain distance before their true relevance can be seen. Literature can both provide new worlds for a student which add to his immediate experience and give him new eyes with which to view the experience he has had. We must remember, however, that what is relevant for one student may not be for another. Books that are truly relevant for students will stretch their minds; and since no two minds are exactly alike, few, if any, books are equally appropriate for every student in a given class.

Some minds are better stretched by certain kinds of books than by others, and the teacher would do well to consider the kind of book that is most likely to reach a particular mind. As we have seen in Part Two, fiction, biography, history, and fantasy fall somewhere along a continuum. Certain teaching approaches work equally well with all of these, although one must be careful not to demand of a work something inappropriate to its generic subclass. As Virginia Woolf reminds us:

It is simple enough to say that since books have classes—
fiction, biography, poetry—we should separate them and take
from each what it is right that each should give us. Yet few
people ask from books what books can give us. Most commonly we come to books with blurred and divided minds, asking of fiction that it shall be true, of poetry that it shall be
false, of biography that it shall be flattering, of history that it
shall enforce our own prejudices. If we could banish all such
preconceptions when we read, that would be an admirable beginning. Do not dictate to your author; try to become him.[3]

Trying to become the author, though it makes one aware of generic
differences, should very soon make one aware of similarities between genres as well. One will come to realize that characterization
is as much an art in biography as in the novel and that it is accomplished in much the same way. The excitement that a writer of
fantasy achieves is not so different from the excitement that a historian may arouse about the events he recounts—*Hiroshima* is not
so very different from *The Red Badge of Courage* in the way that
each engages the reader and adds to the annals of history—whether
the narrative be real or imagined. Indeed, differences within a
genre may be as great as those between certain representatives of
different genres. Thus the differences between biography as a form
and the novel as a form may not be as significant as those between,
on the one hand, a biography that is rambling and unselective, and
one in which the materials are chosen carefully to contribute to a
unified theme; or, on the other hand, a novel, like *David Copperfield,* which simply provides a kind of history of the hero's life,
and a novel, like *Great Expectations,* which gives that history within
the context of a theme which shapes the progress of the narrative
and controls the process of selection. Many of the questions, then,
that can be asked of biography as a literary form can also be asked
of fiction, and some of these questions, in turn, may be applied to
works of history or fantasy. Young readers may be engaged with
history and its "characters," just as they may be led to see that
beyond the events in fiction may lie historical or universal truths.

Designing a unit

There are, however, two major problems in using any of these
books: their length represents a major commitment of class time

3. Virginia Woolf, "How Should One Read a Book?" *The Second Common Reader* (New York:
Harcourt Brace Jovanovich, Inc., 1932), p. 282.

and student energy, and the enormous range in talent and interest within any class makes it unlikely that a single book will appeal equally to all. Rather than search for those few books which might appeal nearly universally to a given class, the teacher might arrange a unit in which individuals and small groups within the class read different works of fiction (and perhaps nonfiction) with different levels of difficulty, but with common themes or of common types. Students might do a certain amount of writing which grows out of their reading; they might engage in small group discussions if scheduling and the physical conditions of the room make this possible; and then all the groups might come together as a class to share some of the experiences that each individual or small group has had. A procedure of this sort might well replace the oral or written book report—a vanishing species, one would hope, in its traditional form. In place of a mere summary of the book (often cribbed from some plot outline), a plan such as that outlined above would provide an opportunity for a selective discussion of some aspect of each book related to the major theme or type of book, and might thus achieve a real sharing of highlights of the books with classmates, inducing them to read additional books for their own pleasure. Such a unit would involve planning by the teacher at three points: first, the preparation of a list of books from which each member of the class, with guidance, might make an appropriate choice; second, orientation of the students for reading—as individuals or in small groups—the books they have chosen; and third, orientation for the reports and class discussion which would follow the reading of the books.

The guiding principle for preparation of a list of books from which students would make choices might be either thematic or generic. Thus ninth- or tenth-grade students might be given a list of books in which there is an element of fantasy: Ray Bradbury's *Fahrenheit 451,* William Golding's *Lord of the Flies,* George Orwell's *Animal Farm,* Saul Bellow's *Henderson the Rain King,* Alexei Panshin's *Rite of Passage,* William Melvin Kelley's *A Different Drummer,* Jonathan Swift's *Gulliver's Travels*—the list might, of course, be extended. The teacher would than guide students so that less sophisticated readers would choose the simpler books like *Animal Farm* or *Fahrenheit 451* or *Rite of Passage,* while somewhat more sophisticated readers would choose *Lord of the Flies* or *A Different Drummer,* and the most experienced readers would choose *Gulliver* or *Henderson the Rain King.*

Another unit, thematic rather than generic, might use a group of books concerned in one way or another with adolescence and the process of growing up. Such a list, again for ninth- or tenth-graders, might contain Conrad Richter's *Light in the Forest,* John Knowles' *A Separate Peace,* Langston Hughes' *Not Without Laughter,* Carson McCullers' *A Member of the Wedding,* Alexei Panshin's *Rite of Passage,* William Faulkner's *Intruder in the Dust,* John Steinbeck's *The Red Pony,* Harper Lee's *To Kill a Mockingbird,* William Golding's *Lord of the Flies,* William Demby's *Beetlecreek,* Charles Dickens' *Great Expectations,* Gordon Parks' *The Learning Tree*—again the list might be extended almost indefinitely. Note, incidentally, that some books appear on both of these lists and might well fit into either context, though the approach might be slightly different depending on the unit in which each is used.

A unit on the black experience

Let me give a more fully developed plan for a thematic unit centered around the black experience in America, and discuss in somewhat more detail the various stages that might go into preparing such a unit, perhaps for eleventh- or twelfth-graders. The teacher planning such a unit is at once faced with a problem analogous to that faced by black writers themselves. Langston Hughes advises a young black writer to be "*writer* first, *colored* second. That means losing nothing of your racial identity," he continues, since

good art transcends land, race or nationality, and color drops away. If you are a good writer, in the end neither blackness nor whiteness makes a difference to readers.

Greek the writer of *Oedipus* might have been, but *Oedipus* shakes Booker T. Washington High School. Irish was Shaw, but he rocks Fisk University. Scottish was Bobby Burns, but kids like him at Tuskegee. The more regional or national an art is in its origins, the more universal it may become in the end. What could be more Spanish than *Don Quixote?* Yet what is more universal? What more Italian than Dante? Or more English than Shakespeare? Advice to Negro writers: Step *outside yourself,* then look back—and you will see how human, yet how beautiful and black, you are. How very black—even when you're integrated.[4]

4. Langston Hughes, "Writers: Black and White" (1959), in *An Introduction to Black Literature in America From 1746 to the Present,* Lindsay Patterson, ed., *International Library of Negro Life and History* (New York: Publisher's Company, Inc., © 1968 by the Association for the Study of Negro Life and History), p. 282.

Loften Mitchell, on the other hand, deplores the fact that "the Negro writer . . . is asked to do something no other writer is asked to do, namely, to forget his cultural heritage and write of something else—something 'universal.' This, of course, implies that the Negro is not human. No one has asked O'Casey to ignore the Irish. No one has told Odets to forget the Jews. No one has told Tennessee Williams to get out of the South."[5] The contradiction between these two passages, of course, lies more in the methods they suggest than in the ultimate outcomes for the writer, and both insist upon the importance of both the universal and the specific. Just as the black writer must somehow achieve a balance between the unique things of his cultural heritage and the universal experiences which lie behind them, the teacher in designing a unit on the black experience will wish to treat the books both as sources of social and cultural insight and as works of literature with universal literary qualities. Since it would probably be easier for students as a class to share what John Knowles calls "the informational side" of the novel[6] than to share their literary experiences, the teacher will probably wish to emphasize ways to enrich that literary experience in the orientation of individuals and groups for their reading, and emphasize informational and thematic elements in orienting the individuals and groups for discussion by the whole class. In the discussion which follows, it is assumed that students will have been trained to look for important literary elements in their reading, such as characterization, point of view, and style.

The teacher who wishes to teach such a unit need not be an authority on black literature, but he must obviously be willing to develop a sufficient background through reading and research to enable him to make intelligent choices about which materials to use and how to guide individual student choices.[7] His first step should be to familiarize himself with all or part of a list of books such as

5. Loften Mitchell, "The Negro Writer and His Materials" (1959), in *An Introduction to Black Literature in America*, p. 285.

6. See p. 153.

7. Helpful guides to reading and research may be found in Darwin T. Turner's NCTE lecture, "The Teaching of Literature by Afro-American Writers," in *The Promise of English: NCTE 1970 Distinguished Lectures* (Champaign, Ill.: National Council of Teachers of English, 1970), pp. 73–98, and his definitive bibliography, *Afro-American Writers* (New York: Appleton-Century-Crofts, 1970). Other helpful guides include Barbara Dodds' *Negro Literature for High School Students* (Champaign, Ill.: National Council of Teachers of English, 1968); and, for elementary and junior high classes, Charlemae Rollins' *We Build Together*, rev. ed. (Champaign, Ill.: National Council of Teachers of English, 1967). The teacher may also wish to acquire a broader historical background by consulting works like John Hope Franklin's *From Slavery to Freedom: A History of Negro Americans*, 3rd ed. (New York: Alfred A. Knopf, Inc., 1967), also available in paperback (New York: Vintage Books, Random House, Inc., 1969); Winthrop D. Jordan's *White over Black* (Chapel Hill, N.C.: University of North Carolina Press, 1968); and Earl Conrad's *The Invention of the Negro* (New York: Paul S. Eriksson, Inc., 1966).

the following, guiding his reading by whatever annotation is available in order to construct a similar list for his particular class:

Angelou, Maya. *I Know Why the Caged Bird Sings.* New York: Random House, Inc., 1969. Autobiography of the childhood in Arkansas and California of a black woman who later became well known as a dancer, writer on Africa, and coordinator in the civil rights movement.

Baldwin, James. *The Fire Next Time.* New York: Dial Press, Inc., 1962. Two autobiographical "letters," discussing what it means to be a Negro in America and suggesting something about the way we may "end the racial nightmare."

———. *Go Tell It on the Mountain.* New York: Alfred A. Knopf, Inc., 1953. Novel describing life in Harlem and the religious experience of a young black boy.

Bontemps, Arna. *Black Thunder.* New York: The Macmillan Company, 1936. Historical novel telling the story of an unsuccessful slave rebellion in 1800; based on historical fact.

Brown, Claude. *Manchild in the Promised Land.* New York: The Macmillan Company, 1965. Autobiography of a Negro who survived all the dangers and destructive forces of the Harlem ghetto to become a law student.

Chesnutt, Charles W. *The Marrow of Tradition.* Boston: Houghton Mifflin Company, 1901. Novel of life in a southern town during Reconstruction which builds to an exciting, if melodramatic, climax.

Cleaver, Eldridge. *Soul on Ice.* New York: McGraw-Hill Book Company, 1968. Autobiography and social analysis by one of the most militant blacks.

Demby, William. *Beetlecreek.* New York: Holt, Rinehart & Winston, Inc., 1950. A first novel describing part of the growing up process of a Negro boy and the failure of a white recluse to escape his own loneliness by trying to bring the black and white races together in a West Virginia town.

Du Bois, W. E. Burghardt. *Darkwater: Voices from Within the Veil.* New York: Harcourt Brace Jovanovich, Inc., 1920. Sketches and essays, some autobiographical, discussing a wide range of topics, often with insights that are surprisingly contemporary. Du Bois, who died in Ghana at the age of ninety-five in 1963, was an outstanding scholar in the fields of history, sociology, and anthropology, as well as being active in the United Nations and world affairs, the NAACP, and the Negro Renaissance in the 1920's and 1930's.

———. *The Souls of Black Folk.* Chicago: A. C. McClurg and Company, 1903. Essays and sketches delineating various aspects of Negro life in the South and opposing the views of Booker T. Washington on ways to improve the lot of the Negro.

Ellison, Ralph. *Invisible Man.* New York: Random House, Inc., 1947. Award-winning novel which describes with much symbolic richness, the journey of a young Negro from the South to the North and from innocence to disillusionment and understanding.

Gaines, Ernest J. *Of Love and Dust.* New York: Dial Press, Inc., 1967. Tragic novel of interracial love on a modern-day Louisiana plantation.

Griffin, John Howard. *Black Like Me.* Boston: Houghton Mifflin Company, 1960. A white writer's account of his experiences when he darkened his skin temporarily by medical treatments and passed as a Negro on a trip through the South.

Hughes, Langston. *Not Without Laughter.* New York: Alfred A. Knopf, Inc., 1930. Novel describing the growing up of a black boy in a small Kansas town in the first quarter of the twentieth century.

Hurston, Zora Neale. *Their Eyes Were Watching God.* New York: J. B. Lippincott Company, 1937. Novel, set in Florida with a devastating hurricane as its climax, describing a black woman's search for love.

Johnson, James Weldon. *The Autobiography of an Ex-Coloured Man.* Boston: Sherman, French and Company, 1912. Novel describing the youth and young manhood of a light-skinned Negro at the turn of the century, who finally decides to cross the color line and pass as white.

Kelley, William Melvin. *A Different Drummer.* New York: Doubleday & Company, Inc., 1959. A first novel describing the private revolt of one Negro which spreads to a whole state.

Killens, John Oliver. *And Then We Heard the Thunder.* New York: Alfred A. Knopf, Inc., 1963. World War II novel describing the struggle of a black GI outfit for a double victory against the Japanese and against discrimination in the Army; the hero is likewise engaged in a personal struggle to determine his relationship to the Army, to the racial question, and to his wife.

———. *Black Man's Burden.* New York: Trident Press, Simon & Schuster, Inc., 1965. Essays, addressed to whites, containing autobiography, analysis, and exhortation; a good companion piece to Baldwin's *The Fire Next Time* (see above).

Malcolm X and Haley, Alex. *The Autobiography of Malcolm X.* New York: Grove Press, Inc., 1964. The true story of the man who rose from the depths of the Harlem ghetto to become one of the leaders in the Black Muslim movement, broke away to found his own organization, and was felled by assassins' bullets.

Marshall, Paule. *Brown Girl, Brownstones.* New York: Random House, Inc., 1959. Novel describing the growing up of a West Indian girl in Brooklyn during the 1930's and 1940's.

McKay, Claude. *Banjo.* New York: Harper & Row, Publishers, 1929. "A story without a plot," describing the lives of a group of Negroes on the Marseilles waterfront during the 1920's.

Parks, Gordon. *The Learning Tree.* New York: Harper & Row, Publishers, 1963. Novel describing the growing up of a black boy in Kansas in roughly the same period as *Not Without Laughter* (see above).

Petry, Ann. *The Street.* Boston: Houghton Mifflin Company, 1946. Tragic novel depicting the struggle of a young black woman to free herself and her eight-year-old son from the destructive forces of the Harlem ghetto.

Schuyler, George S. *Black No More.* New York: Macaulay Company, 1931. Fantasy describing what happens when a process for turning black skin white is discovered, and satirizing both black and white attitudes and institutions.

Scott, William Walter III. *Hurt, Baby, Hurt.* Ann Arbor, Mich.: New Ghetto Press, Inc., 1970. A young Negro's autobiographical account of growing up in Detroit, climaxed by his experiences at the time of the Detroit riot in 1967.

Thomas, Piri. *Down These Mean Streets.* New York: Alfred A. Knopf, Inc., 1967. Autobiography of a Puerto Rican who grew up in Spanish Harlem; interesting to compare with Brown's *Manchild in the Promised Land* (see above).

Thurman, Wallace. *The Blacker the Berry.* New York: Macaulay Company, 1929. Novel of the twenties describing the bitterness of its dark-skinned heroine at discrimination she suffers from those with lighter skins.

Walker, Margaret. *Jubilee.* Boston: Houghton Mifflin Company, 1966. Historical novel, set in Georgia in the Civil War era, depicting the life of a young black woman both as a slave and as a freed woman; an interesting companion piece to *Gone with the Wind.*

Williams, John A. *Sissie.* New York: Farrar, Straus, and Cudahy, Inc., 1963. Novel depicting the struggles of a very human black woman to exist, and the effects of these struggles on the lives of her children.

———. *Sons of Darkness, Sons of Light.* Boston: Little, Brown and

Company, 1969. A dramatic and absorbing novel, set in the future, depicting events which follow the murder of a white policeman who had killed a black youth and which culminate in an all-out race war.

———. *This Is My Country Too.* New York: The New American Library, Inc., 1965. Narrative of a trip around the United States taken by black author John Williams during the early sixties; might make an interesting comparison with *Black Like Me* (see above).

Wright, Richard. *Black Boy.* New York: Harper & Row, Publishers, 1937. Autobiography describing the southern childhood of one of the best known black novelists.

———. *Native Son.* New York: Harper & Row, Publishers, 1940. The violent story of Bigger Thomas, inhabitant of the Chicago ghetto; a classic American *Crime and Punishment.*

Yerby, Frank. *Speak Now.* New York: Dial Press, Inc., 1969. Novel, set in contemporary Paris, depicting the love between a black jazz musician, veteran of Vietnam, and a southern white girl.

All of these writers (with the exception of Griffin) are black; all of the books are currently available in paperback (although one must remember that paperback editions go in and out of print with some suddenness). If the teacher wishes to expand the list with some hardcover additions, he might consider such titles as Ronald L. Fair's *Hog Butcher* (New York: Harcourt Brace Jovanovich, Inc., 1966), the story of a courageous black boy in Chicago who defies the police department to tell the truth about a killing he has seen; Julian Mayfield's *The Hit* (New York: Vanguard Press, Inc., 1957), describing a day in the life of a family in Harlem and centering around the father's dreams of acquiring sudden wealth; or Toni Morrison's *The Bluest Eye* (New York: Holt, Rinehart & Winston, Inc., 1970), a poetic and compelling novel describing the lives of some black children and the people around them in an Ohio town in the early 1940's. These may well appear in paperback soon. References to novels like Alan Paton's *Cry, the Beloved Country* and E. M. Forster's *A Passage to India,* though these are not by black writers, might enable the teacher to draw upon students' past reading and make comparisons with books from other countries.

The teacher's first step, then, would be to expand or contract some such list as the one given, expanding it as his interests and knowledge suggest, and contracting it to fit the particular situation of his class and community. Some of these books may not be appropriate in some classes or communities, particularly because of the frankness of their language. The fact that any single book would be optional reading rather than required for the whole class may help to solve any problems of this sort. More important, in making up a final list the teacher will want to take into account both the student's interests (unusual motivation can sometimes make up for less sophisticated reading ability), and the level of his reading sophistication. Since the list contains novels, autobiographies, and collections of essays, the student's preference for one or another of these forms might also be taken into account. The teacher will want to guide students so that only the more sophisticated choose the books which are more difficult in one way or another, books like *Go Tell It on the Mountain* or *Invisible Man.* Finally, the teacher's own background and the nature of the class will also enter into the choices. A black teacher and a white teacher may be comfortable adopting somewhat different stances toward these materials. Black students may develop a sense of racial pride from a unit such as this, while white students may find their knowledge increased and their sympathies widened by the unit. At the same time there is the danger that some of these books may be old stories to black students, and that some of them may appear to white students to be too didactic or propagandistic. Though in the discussion which follows I shall refer to many (though not all) of these books, it is obviously easy enough for the teacher to drop out any book or, in some cases, to use a passage or two from a book which is not to be read as a whole.

Orientation for reading. Orientation of the class before the reading begins should stress two kinds of things: first, the ways in which individual readers can get the most out of each book; and second, the kinds of things that students should be prepared to share with the whole class later in discussion. In suggesting ways for students to get inside the book they have chosen and get the most out of it, the teacher might make the distinction between putting oneself in the same situation as the character in the book and putting oneself inside the character. It is always easier to put yourself in someone else's shoes than to put yourself in his skin; yet it is important for students to do both. Thus they should be led constantly to ask themselves two different questions as they read: What would I do if I were in his place? How would I feel if I were he? Discussion by the whole class of the distinction between putting oneself in another's shoes and in another's skin should help to prepare students to respond individually to the books they read.

Students should also be asked to put themselves in the place of their classmates as they prepare for the final report and discussion with the class as a whole. What would their classmates like to know about the book in order to decide whether they would like to read it themselves? What would they enjoy about it most? What might they learn from it? After questions like these have been asked and answered, then students should be ready to prepare brief summaries of important aspects of the book (scenes, themes, characters, etc.) and to choose brief passages from the book to be shared with the class as a kickoff for discussion.

Students may also find that a certain amount of writing helps them to answer the questions we have been talking about. They might be urged to keep informal journals with comments centering on those questions or perhaps write short papers on one sharply focused aspect of what they are reading. Another kind of writing assignment that might aid in interpretation of selected key passages is suggested by an excerpt from Richard Wright's *Black Boy.* Students might be asked to add the kind of interpretative comment that Wright supplies below to some other passage from a book they are reading:

"Man, them white folks sure is mean." Complaining.

"That's how come so many colored folks leaving the South." Informational.

"And, man, they sure hate for you to leave." Pride of personal and racial worth implied.

"Yeah. They wanna keep you here and work you to death."

"The first white sonofabitch that bothers me is gonna get a hole knocked in his head!" Naive rebellion.

"That ain't gonna do you no good. Hell, they'll catch you." Rejection of naive rebellion.

"Ha-ha-ha . . . Yeah, goddammit, they really catch you, now." Appreciation of the thoroughness of white militancy.

"Yeah, white folks set on their white asses day and night, but leta nigger do something, and they get every bloodhound that was ever born and put 'em on his trail." Bitter pride in realizing what it costs to defeat them. . . .

"Man, what makes white folks so mean?" Returning to grapple with the old problem.

"Whenever I see one I spit." Emotional rejection of whites.

"Man, ain't they ugly?" Increased emotional rejection.

"Man, you ever get right close to a white man, close enough to smell 'im?" Anticipation of statement.

"They say we stink. But my ma says white folks smell like dead folks." Wishing the enemy was dead.

"Niggers smell from sweat. But white folks smell *all* the time." The enemy is an animal to be killed on sight.

And the talk would weave, roll, surge, spurt, veer, swell, having no specific aim or direction, touching vast areas of life, expressing the tentative impulses of childhood.[8]

This technique might be used in a small group as the basis for discussion as students compare and discuss the interpretations they have written for a given passage.

A variation on this exercise, likewise designed to help students to interpret and appreciate particular passages, is suggested by a conversation in Toni Morrison's *The Bluest Eye,* which two children overhear as their mother tells her friends about a new roomer:

"I kind of thought Henry would marry her one of these days."
"That old woman?"
"Well, Henry ain't no chicken."
"No, but he ain't no buzzard, either."
"He ever been married to anybody?"
"No."
"How come? Somebody cut it off?"
"He's just picky."
"He ain't picky. You see anything around here you'd marry?"
"Well . . . no."
"He's just sensible. A steady worker with quiet ways. I hope it works out all right."
"It will. How much you charging?"
"Five dollars every two weeks."
"That'll be a big help to you."
"I'll say."

Their conversation is like a gently wicked dance: sound meets sound, curtsies, shimmies, and retires. Another sound enters but is upstaged by still another: the two circle each other and stop. Sometimes their words move in lofty spirals; other times they take strident leaps, and all of it is punctuated with warm-pulsed laughter—like the throb of a heart made of jelly. The edge, the curl, the thrust of their emotions is always clear to Frieda and me. We do not, cannot, know the meanings of all their words, for we are nine and ten years old. So we watch their faces, their hands, their feet, and listen for truth in timbre.[9]

8. Richard Wright, *Black Boy* (New York: Harper & Row, Publishers, 1945), Ch. 3, pp. 69–71.
9. Toni Morrison, *The Bluest Eye* (New York: Holt, Rinehart & Winston, Inc., 1970), pp. 9–10.

Students might be invited to find a scene in which there is conversation, which the author has presented without summarizing comment, and write the same sort of interpretation of it that is found at the end of the passage above. A specific point of view for the interpretation—note that it is that of the two children in this passage—might likewise be suggested.

Still another writing exercise, based on point of view, might be developed from this passage in Ann Petry's *The Street,* describing an incident which Lutie, the heroine, has seen. A crowd has gathered on the sidewalk:

> There was a cleared space near the buildings and a handful of policemen and cameramen and reporters with pink cards stuck in their hatbands were standing in it looking down at something. She got as close to the cleared space as she could—so close that she was almost touching the policeman in front of her.
>
> And she saw what they were looking at. Lying flat on the sidewalk was a man—thin, shabby, tall from the amount of sidewalk that his body occupied. There was blood on the sidewalk, and she saw that it was coming from somewhere under him. Part of his body and his face were covered with what looked to be a piece of white canvas.
>
> But the thing she had never been able to forget were his shoes. Only the uppers were intact. They had once been black, but they were now a dark dull gray from long wear. The soles were worn out. They were mere flaps attached to the uppers. She could see the layers of wear. The first outer layer of leather was left near the edges, and then the great gaping holes in the center where the leather had worn out entirely, so that for weeks he must have walked practically barefooted on the pavement. . . .

[The victim's sister comes and identifies the body; Lutie is shocked at the girl's sense of resignation. Then she pushes her way to the back of the crowd and asks what has happened to the man.]

> A woman with a bundle of newspapers under her arm answered her. She shifted the papers from one arm to the other. "White man in the baker shop killed him with a bread knife."
>
> There was a silence, and then another voice added: "He had the bread knife in him and he walked to the corner. The cops brought him back here and he died there where he's layin' now."

"White man in the store claims he tried to hold him up."

"If that bastard white man puts one foot out here, we'll kill him. Cops or no cops."

She went home remembering, not the threat of violence in that silent, waiting crowd, but instead the man's ragged sole- less shoes and the resigned look on the girl's face. She had never been able to forget either of them. The boy was so thin—painfully thin—and she kept thinking about his walking through the city barefooted. Both he and his sister were so young.

The next day's papers said that a "burly Negro" had failed in his effort to hold up a bakery shop, for the proprietor had surprised him by resisting and stabbed him with a bread knife. She held the paper in her hand for a long time, trying to follow the reasoning by which that thin ragged boy had become in the eyes of a reporter a "burly Negro." And she decided that it all depended on where you sat how these things looked. If you looked at them from inside the framework of a fat weekly salary, and you thought of colored people as naturally criminal, then you didn't really see what any Negro looked like. You couldn't, because the Negro was never an individual. He was a threat, or an animal, or a curse, or a blight, or a joke.[10]

After discussion of the differences between the points of view of Lutie, the crowd, and the reporter in this passage, students might be asked to choose another brief dramatic passage or vignette from the book they are reading and retell it from a point of view different from that which the author has adopted—perhaps a reporter's, per- haps that of another character, perhaps their own imaginative pro- jection. Exercises of this sort—performed either by small groups or by the class as a whole after they have studied a brief passage— should help students not only in their reading of their own in- dividual books, but also in the understanding of the central theme for the unit, which will often depend upon an understanding of the point of view.

Orientation for studying theme. Both in orienting students for their work as individuals or members of small groups and in prepar- ing for the full class discussion which will follow, the teacher, as has been said, must achieve a balance between viewing the books as the sources for ideas and viewing the books as the sources of literary experiences for the students. Since this unit, because of its

10. Ann Petry, *The Street* (Boston: Houghton Mifflin Company, 1946), Ch. 8, pp. 195–196, 198–199.

nature, will inevitably contain temptations to stress certain elements of history and sociology as well as those of a more purely literary sort, it might be well before going any further to make some distinctions—oversimplified though they may be—between the typical approach to a literary theme and the typical approach to a historical or sociological theme. The social sciences aim at objective truth about man's past and the nature of his social institutions; they use research techniques which yield data that may then be interpreted and formed into final conclusions by using the canons of logic. In general, the social sciences place less emphasis on the individual, except insofar as the individual may constitute a representative case. One comes away from reading a book of history or sociology asking the question, "What has this taught me?" One may also question what he can do about a particular problem or situation that has been described. Literature, in contrast to the social sciences, usually places more emphasis upon the individual than upon society, and almost always upon the individual as important and interesting in himself, though seen, of course, in a particular social context. One demands of literature, particularly when viewing it from its thematic aspect, that it convince by its manner of presentation as well as by the matter presented. In other words, in literature we look for a kind of esthetic truth as well as philosophical, historical, or sociological truth. One comes away from reading a work of literature asking, "What has this told me about the human condition in the particular context it has chosen?" and "What is the relationship of that context to other human contexts?" Like the work of literature, the work of the social scientist should have some esthetic value if it is to please the reader; and like the work of the social scientist, the work of literature may provide the reader with fresh information and lead him to question what action he can take on a particular problem presented. But the prime fidelity of the social scientist must remain to objective, historical, sociological truth, while the prime loyalty of the literary artist is to imaginative, esthetic, human truth.

If one accepts these rather rough distinctions, certain corollaries follow. The concern of students in reading literature should be directed to the presentation of the individual within the thematic framework, and to the question of whether that individual has acted believably in believable situations; whereas in the study of history or sociology, students should be led to place more emphasis upon the accumulation of evidence and the interpretation of fact. This is not to say that a work of literature may not ultimately be as powerful an incentive to human action as a work of sociology—indeed, it can be an even more powerful incentive, just as an account of a starving family can be a more emotionally persuasive argument for increased welfare payments than a statistical table giving the incomes of poor families. But at its best, literature persuades to action because the issues that it presents are seen against the backdrop of a larger collection of human values, and it is with this knowledge firmly in mind that the teacher should approach the thematic implications of this unit.

One of the literary realities of which students should be most aware as they work toward an understanding of themes is tone. Tone may be defined as one manifestation of point of view:[11] it is the linguistic result of the attitude a writer or speaker adopts. In conversation it inheres in the tone of the voice as much as in the actual words; in writing, the author must find a way in words to approximate the tones of the voice. Proper assessment of tone is necessary to the understanding of meaning, since the same words can convey quite different meanings, depending on the tone of a larger context. The books that students will be reading in this unit provide a wide variety of tones; and in general, the contrasts in tones are not related to any generic distinctions between fiction and nonfiction: much the same range of tones is available to the writer of each kind of book.

Students should be encouraged to make comparisons between the tones of passages like these (chosen, in this case, to represent a difference of attitude about a similar subject). In the first, William Walter Scott is describing his feelings about the organized religion of some "middle-class" blacks:

> I couldn't be in that bag because like when they came to church I saw then they didn't come to pray. They came to wallow in their own self-hatred. I mean they were different from the usual church-going hypocrite. More screwed-up. You know it seemed they were coming to church to ask God to forgive them for being black. . . .
>
> I mean like when the plate was passed up and down through the aisles that was the only time you felt you were in communion with God and church and other people:
>
> "Rejoice, rejoice, ye pure in heart, I put more money in than you this week. And everyone saw me too. I'm saved, I'm saved. I gave. I paid this Sunday like the others for the freedom of my body . . . and my soul. . . ."
>
> I stopped going to church and started to work with myself.

---

11. See the discussion of point of view in Part Two.

Like if I had a need to pray, from that day to this, I just sort of look up in the sky and say man you know me and you know who I am and I'm in a little trouble down here and I need a helping hand. Amen. And I believe that and so I let it go and let the Lord handle it from up there and I deal with it from down here.

So the Lord's good for something if you take him out of that crazy status-symbol church-going race. Besides, for all I know, God doesn't exist.[12]

In this passage from Langston Hughes' *Not Without Laughter* a group of characters discuss religion. Harriet, Hager's daughter, has just been telling her mother and Mrs. Johnson, a neighbor, about her new job:

"Long's it keeps you off de streets, I's glad," said Hager, rocking contentedly. "Maybe I can git you goin' to church agin now."

"Aw, I don't like church," the girl replied.

"An', chile, I can't blame you much," said Sister Johnson, fumbling in the pocket of her apron. "De way dese churches done got now'days. . . . Sandy, run in de house an' ask yo' pappy fo' a match to light ma pipe. . . . It ain't 'Come to Jesus' no mo' a-tall. Ministers dese days an' times don't care nothin' 'bout po' Jesus. 'Stead o' dat it's rally dis an' collection dat, an' de aisle wants a new carpet, an' de pastor needs a 'lectric fan fer his red-hot self." The old sister spat into the yard. "Money! That's all 'tis! An' white folkses' religion—Lawd help! 'Taint no use in mentionin' them."

"True," agreed Hager.

"'Cause if de gates o' heaven shuts in white folkses' faces like de do's o' dey church in us niggers' faces, it'll be too bad! Yes, sir! One thing sho, de Lawd ain't prejudiced!"

"No," said Hager; "but He don't love ugly, neither in niggers nor in white folks."[13]

In this passage, Claude Brown describes his father's "religion":

Even though Dad didn't care for preachers and churches, he

12. William Walter Scott, III, *Hurt, Baby, Hurt* (Ann Arbor, Mich.: New Ghetto Press Inc., 1970), pp. 67–69.
13. Langston Hughes, *Not Without Laughter* (New York: Alfred A. Knopf, Inc., 1930), Ch. 7, pp. 74–75.

had a lot of religion in his own way. Most of the time, his religion didn't show. But on Saturday night, those who didn't see it heard it. Sometimes Dad would get religious on Friday nights too. But Saturday night was a must. Because it always took liquor to start Dad to singing spirituals and talking about the Lord, I thought for years that this lordly feeling was something in a bottle of whiskey. To me, it was like castor oil or black draught. You drink it and the next thing you know, you're doing things.

I was introduced to religion on Saturday night. I don't recall just when, but as far back as I can remember, Saturday night was the Lord's night in our house. Whenever Dad was able to make it home on his own two feet, he would bring a recording of a spiritual, a plate of pigs' feet and potato salad from the corner delicatessen or a plate of fish-and-chips from the wine joint around the corner, and whatever was left of his last bottle of religion. He usually got home about three o'clock in the morning, and the moment he hit the block I could hear him singing (or yelling) the record he had. By the time he got upstairs, everybody in the building knew the song and hated it. Before Dad was in the house, I could hear him calling me.

By the time he finished unlocking and relocking the door at least six times, kicking on it, cursing out the lock and the neighbors who had tried to quiet him down, I was up and had already turned on the phonograph. On her way to the door, Mama would say, "Boy, turn that thing off and git back in that bed." While Mama told Dad how disgusting he was, I would be busily picking out the pigs' feet or fish-and-chips with the least amount of hot sauce on them. When Mama had gotten tired of competing with Dad's singing, she went back to bed. . . . After listening to the record at least a dozen times, Dad would turn the phonograph off, and we would sing the song a few times. Before dawn started sneaking through the windows, Dad and I had gone through his entire repertoire of spirituals. By daybreak, we were both drunk and had fallen on the floor, and we stayed there until we awoke later in the day.

When Dad awoke on Sunday, it was usually around eleven or twelve o'clock. If he had half a bottle of religion around, we would continue our Sunday singing. . . .

Saturdays and Sundays were the only days that Dad mentioned the words "God" and "Lord." But on these days, he made up for the rest of the week. He was very serious about the spirituals and the Lord on weekends. To his way of thinking, this was a private kind of religion all his own. Nobody understood except him and the Lord, but that was enough understanding for him.[14]

This passage from Maya Angelou, like the one above from Brown, is humorous in tone; yet the humor and the perspective are different:

Once when [Sister Monroe] hadn't been to church for a few months (she had taken off to have a child), she got the spirit and started shouting, throwing her arms around and jerking her body, so that the ushers went over to hold her down, but she tore herself away from them and ran up to the pulpit. She stood in front of the altar, shaking like a freshly caught trout. She screamed at Reverend Taylor. "Preach it. I say, preach it." Naturally he kept on preaching as if she wasn't standing there telling him what to do. Then she screamed an extremely fierce "I said, preach it" and stepped up on the altar. The Reverend kept on throwing out phrases like home-run balls and Sister Monroe made a quick break and grasped for him. For just a second, everything and everyone in the church except Reverend Taylor and Sister Monroe hung loose like stockings on a washline. Then she caught the minister by the sleeve of his jacket and his coattail, then she rocked him from side to side.

I have to say this for our minister, he never stopped giving us the lesson. The usher board made its way to the pulpit, going up both aisles with a little more haste than is customarily seen in church. Truth to tell, they fairly ran to the minister's aid. Then two of the deacons, in their shiny Sunday suits, joined the ladies in white on the pulpit, and each time they pried Sister Monroe loose from the preacher he took another deep breath and kept on preaching, and Sister Monroe grabbed him in another place, and more firmly. Reverend Taylor was helping his rescuers as much as possible by jumping around when he got a chance. His voice at one point got so low it sounded like a roll of thunder, then Sister Monroe's "Preach it" cut through the roar, and we all wondered (I did, in any case) if it would ever end. Would they go on forever, or get tired out at last like a game of blindman's bluff that lasted too long, with nobody caring who was "it"?

I'll never know what might have happened, because magi-

---

14. Claude Brown, *Manchild in the Promised Land* (New York: The Macmillan Company, 1965), Ch. 1, pp. 27–28.

cally the pandemonium spread. The spirit infused Deacon Jackson and Sister Willson, the chairman of the usher board, at the same time. Deacon Jackson, a tall, thin, quiet man, who was also a part-time Sunday school teacher, gave a scream like a falling tree, leaned back on thin air and punched Reverend Taylor on the arm. It must have hurt as much as it caught the Reverend unawares. There was a moment's break in the rolling sounds and Reverend Taylor jerked around surprised, and hauled off and punched Deacon Jackson. In the same second Sister Willson caught his tie, looped it over her fist a few times, and pressed down on him. There wasn't time to laugh or cry before all three of them were down on the floor behind the altar. Their legs spiked out like kindling wood.

Sister Monroe, who had been the cause of all the excitement, walked off the dais, cool and spent, and raised her flinty voice in the hymn, "I came to Jesus, as I was, worried, wound, and sad, I found in Him a resting place and He has made me glad."

The minister took advantage of already being on the floor and asked in a choky little voice if the church would kneel with him to offer a prayer of thanksgiving. He said we had been visited with a mighty spirit, and let the whole church say Amen.

On the next Sunday, he took his text from the eighteenth chapter of the Gospel according to St. Luke, and talked quietly but seriously about the Pharisees, who prayed in the streets so that the public would be impressed with their religious devotion. I doubt that anyone got the message—certainly not those to whom it was directed. The deacon board, however, did appropriate funds for him to buy a new suit. The other was a total loss.[15]

The final selection, taken from James Baldwin's *Go Tell It on the Mountain,* describes a scene after an all-night church service at which Johnny has been "saved" (Johnny's father is a "deacon" or lay preacher):

Then he stood before his father. In the moment that he forced himself to raise his eyes and look into his father's face, he felt in himself a stiffening, and a panic, and a blind rebellion, and a hope for peace. The tears still on his face, and smiling still, he said: "Praise the Lord."

15. Maya Angelou, *I Know Why the Caged Bird Sings* (New York: Random House, Inc., 1969), Ch. 6, pp. 38–40.

"Praise the Lord," said his father. He did not move to touch him, did not kiss him, did not smile. They stood before each other in silence, while the saints rejoiced; and John struggled to speak the authoritative, the living word that would conquer the great division between his father and himself. But it did not come, the living word; in the silence something died in John, and something came alive. It came to him that he must testify: his tongue only could bear witness to the wonders he had seen. And he remembered, suddenly, the text of a sermon he had once heard his father preach. And he opened his mouth, feeling, as he watched his father, the darkness roar behind him, and the very earth beneath him seem to shake; yet he gave to his father their common testimony. "I'm saved," he said, "and I know I'm saved." And then, as his father did not speak, he repeated his father's text: "My witness is in Heaven and my record is on high."

"It come from your mouth," said his father then, "I want to see you live it. It's more than a notion."

"I'm going to pray God," said John—and his voice shook, whether with joy or grief he could not say—"to keep me, and make me strong . . . to stand . . . to stand against the enemy . . . and against everything and everybody . . . that wants to cut down my soul."[16]

The teacher may well have to choose these passages, although students, if they were asked to choose passages dealing with a particular topic—in this case attitudes toward religion—might come up with a similar set. The point, of course, is to choose a set of passages that has some diversity of tones and then to ask students to compare them, characterizing the different tones and noting the differences in effect. In the passages quoted above the range is from the bitterness of Scott to the amused tolerance of Brown; from the boisterous humor of Angelou to the impassioned seriousness of Baldwin; from the underlying skepticism of Scott and Brown to the underlying faith of Hughes and Baldwin; and within the same passage from Hughes, from the sarcastic and complaining remarks of Sister Johnson to the serenity and seriousness of Hager's replies. Discussion of these variations in tone should help students to assess the characters of the speaker and the people described in each passage and to make comparisons of such things as the father-son relationships in Brown and Baldwin, the attacks on the commercial

---

16. James Baldwin, *Go Tell It on the Mountain* (Alfred A. Knopf, Inc., 1953), Part 3, pp. 281–282.

attitude toward religion in Scott and Hughes, the sources and character of the humor in Brown and Angelou, and so on.

Another literary reality that is helpful in the understanding of theme is symbol. Obviously, an exploration of the complex maze of symbols of light and darkness, white and black, seeing and blindness, and dreaming and waking is essential to understanding Ralph Ellison's *Invisible Man,* but less complex books also rely on symbols. In Arna Bontemps' *Black Thunder* the torrential downpour that is largely responsible for the failure of Gabriel's abortive slave revolt is more than a mere backdrop. Starting out on his enterprise, Gabriel denies that the rain is a bad sign and defies the thunder and lightning. After the failure of the revolt, Gabriel says, "The rain was against us. . . . It was a bad night for such doings as we was counting on. A nachal man can't beat the weather, though. . . . Heap of black mens could of been free in this state, only that big rain come up. Befo' God, it looked to me like the sky was emptying plum bottomside up. Excusing that, niggers would of gone free as rabbits."[17] The rain has become significant as a kind of symbolic agent of fate. Similarly, in Gordon Parks' *The Learning Tree,* the anthill that Newt Winger is watching at the beginning of the book is more than just another part of the landscape. Newt's father thinks of the ant as a symbol of energy and hard work. For Newt the anthill and its inhabitants are one more of the wonders of the earth, wonders which he is hungry to explore. As a tornado is about to strike, the winds blow the hill apart, but Newt places his body over the hill to try to protect the ants from the wind until the neighbor girl yanks him to his feet and pulls him toward the safety of a shed. Later in the book, Newt talks with his white friend Rodney Cavanaugh about the habits of ants as they look through Rodney's microscope. Rodney has a store of scientific information but is frankly admiring when Newt tells him that he once counted almost two hundred ants at one time without the aid of a magnifying glass. Near the end of the book Marcus Savage, who has a grudge against Newt and tries to kill him, "plucked a small ant crawling over his knee, held it for a moment, watching it wiggle helplessly; then his powerful black fingers rubbed it into nothingness." If students are asked to spot those places in the book where ants are mentioned, and to put them together, they should be able to see something more about the human beings in the book and their relationships.

    Other kinds of questions that will help focus students' attention

17. Arna Bontemps, *Black Thunder* (New York: The Macmillan Company, 1936), Bk. 2, Ch. 1, p. 106 and Bk. 5, Ch. 2, p. 263.

on the literary qualities of these books might include those calling for speculation on how the books would be changed if their genre or their narrators were changed. For example, how would the autobiographies differ if they were to be made into novels? What would be left out, what would be changed in emphasis, what might be invented by way of supplement? Likewise, in a book like Kelley's *A Different Drummer,* what would the effect be if these different narrators were to tell each other's stories? What can a reader deduce about the characters in an autobiographical or a fictional narrative—and are the possibilities different in each case? If some students can be persuaded to read both, is Baldwin the author of *The Fire Next Time* different from Baldwin the author of *Go Tell It on the Mountain?* Questions like these, to be considered as students read their various books, should likewise help them when they come together with the rest of the class to share their reading experiences and discuss the theme of the unit as a whole, since thematic elements are never entirely separable from the ways in which those themes are expressed.

Orientation for class discussion. The third step, preparation for the full class discussion of the theme of the unit and the different ways that theme has been worked out, should proceed naturally from the work that individuals and small groups have been doing. The danger here, of course, is that discussion by the whole class may turn into a kind of chaos, a series of book reports unrelated to each other. Careful preparation by the teacher—both tactical and logistic—should enable the class to avoid this danger. Discussion by the class as a whole can have common ground if the most eminently shareable elements of the books are discussed and especially if students have some dittoed passages available as a basis for their discussion. It has already been suggested that it is easier to share "information" than to share the other aspects of literary experience, but nonetheless students can give each other an idea of characters, a notion of theme, and—with the help of specific passages—an idea of an author's style. Brief, judiciously chosen passages may help to focus discussion of other aspects of the books as well. Major questions that students should have been asking throughout their reading include these: What does each book tell us about the black experience? How does each book present its themes? how does each book affect you? Do you find the story believable? Do you identify with the author or narrator or main characters? Has each book supported its thematic statements convincingly?

Students in each small group should be urged insofar as possible to foresee the questions that members of the whole class may put to them and to select the passages and the elements in the book they have read that will be of most interest to their classmates. Then discussion by the full class, after the study of different books by individuals and small groups, should begin with a clear statement of purpose. The teacher can explain that the variety of books should enable the class as a whole to arrive at some understanding of the nature of the black experience in America and to proceed to a discussion of the issues and problems which the nature of that experience suggests, together with the various interpretations and solutions which have been proposed, particularly by black writers. The teacher should also point out that understanding of the themes of the unit depends not only upon an understanding of ideas in the books but also upon experiencing the books as works of literature—upon testing them emotionally and esthetically as well as intellectually.

All of the students in the class, whatever book they have read, should be able to reply to such questions as: How has the experience of blacks in America been different from that of whites? What are the things in the black experience that have had most influence on the lives of blacks? What has discrimination meant as far as blacks are concerned? Students will probably point first of all to the very obvious examples of direct cruelty of whites to blacks, ranging all the way from reluctance to serve blacks in a bar,[18] to the "hate stare" that John Howard Griffin received from whites whenever he tried to enter what they considered to be "their world," to the lynching at the end of Du Bois's short sketch, "Of the Coming of John."[19] Other examples of white cruelty may be found in the battle royal incident in Chapter One of Ellison's *Invisible Man* and the comparable incidents in Chapter Twelve of *Black Boy,* when Wright and Harrison are manipulated into distrusting each other and finally fighting for the pleasure of the white audience. With these one might compare the incident in *Manchild in the Promised Land,* in which, though Brown is pushed into a fight by black adults, the atmosphere surrounding the fight is very different and the conclusion likewise of a very different sort. Brown, though reluctant to fight, undertakes to do so as part of the code he lives by; and he ends up becoming fast friends with his opponent.[20] In Ellison and Wright, on the other hand, the incidents form a part of the general atmosphere of fear which whites create for blacks. Wright gives a good example of this fear when he recounts the flight of his mother and aunt after the killing of his uncle, and if students have not chosen this passage to share with the class the teacher might point to it:

18. See, for example, James Baldwin, *The Fire Next Time* (New York: Dial Press, Inc., 1963), "Down at the Cross," pp. 69–70.
19. W. E. B. Du Bois, *The Souls of Black Folk* (Chicago: A. C. McClurg and Company, 1903), Ch. 13.
20. Brown, *Manchild in the Promised Land,* Ch. 10, pp. 253–254.

Fear drowned out grief and that night we packed clothes and dishes and loaded them into a farmer's wagon. Before dawn we were rolling away, fleeing for our lives. I learned afterwards that Uncle Hoskins had been killed by whites who had long coveted his flourishing liquor business. He had been threatened with death and warned many times to leave, but he had wanted to hold on a while longer to amass more money. We got rooms in West Helena, and Aunt Maggie and my mother kept huddled in the house all day and night, afraid to be seen on the streets. Finally Aunt Maggie defied her fear and made frequent trips back to Elaine, but she went in secret and at night and would tell no one save my mother when she was going.

There was no funeral. There was no music. There was no period of mourning. There were no flowers. There were only silence, quiet weeping, whispers, and fear. I did not know when or where Uncle Hoskins was buried. Aunt Maggie was not even allowed to see his body nor was she able to claim any of his assets. Uncle Hoskins had simply been plucked from our midst and we, figuratively, had fallen on our faces to avoid looking into that white-hot face of terror that we knew loomed somewhere above us. This was as close as white terror had ever come to me and my mind reeled. Why had we not fought back, I asked my mother, and the fear that was in her made her slap me into silence.[21]

An even more vicious example of white cruelty can be seen in Charles W. Chesnutt's *The Marrow of Tradition,* written at the turn of the century. McBane, a white supremacist, is trying to incite a lynching after Mrs. Ochiltree, a white woman, has been murdered:

"Burn the nigger," reiterated McBane. "We seem to have the right nigger, but whether we have or not, burn *a* nigger. It is an assault upon the white race, in the person of old Mrs. Ochiltree, committed by the black race, in the person of some nigger. It would justify the white people in burning *any* nigger. The example would be all the more powerful if we got the wrong one. It would serve notice on the niggers that we shall hold the whole race responsible for the misdeeds of each individual."[22]

Another passage of this sort is to be found in Langston Hughes' *Not Without Laughter,* in which a character describes the burning by

21. Wright, *Black Boy,* Ch. 2, p. 48.
22. Charles W. Chesnutt, *The Marrow of Tradition* (Boston: Houghton Mifflin Company, 1901), Ch. 21, p. 182.

whites of a Negro town whose inhabitants had become too prosperous and were "livin' like white folks."[23] These incidents belong to the early part of the century, but fifty years later William Scott describes a comparable terror when he and other blacks are crowded into a garage and held there for hours by the police during the Detroit riot of 1967 and kept in other makeshift jails, including buses, for a week before being arraigned in court. "They don't consider us human," Scott says. "We are animals to them; we have to be tamed, our spirits must be broken."[24]

But, as John A. Williams says, "For a Negro the face of the enemy is varied—all sizes and shapes and colors, even black. Often there is no face at all, but an attitude. . . ."[25] Thus students should recognize in many of these books a second, more subtle, yet even more destructive kind of cruelty that Negroes have suffered. Du Bois described it well at the turn of the century. The Negro, he says, is forced to live in

> a world which yields him no true self-consciousness, but only lets him see himself through the revelation of the other world. It is a peculiar sensation, this double-consciousness, this sense of always looking at one's self through the eyes of others, of measuring one's soul by the tape of a world that looks on in amused contempt and pity. One ever feels his twoness—an American, a Negro; two souls, two thoughts, two unreconciled strivings; two warring ideals in one dark body, whose dogged strength alone keeps it from being torn asunder.
>
> The history of the American Negro is the history of this strife—this longing to attain self-conscious manhood, to merge his double self into a better and truer self. In this merging he wishes neither of the older selves to be lost. He would not Africanize America, for America has too much to teach the world and Africa. He would not bleach his Negro soul in a flood of white Americanism, for he knows that Negro blood has a message for the world. He simply wishes to make it possible for a man to be both a Negro and an American, without being cursed and spit upon by his fellows, without having the doors of Opportunity closed roughly in his face.[26]

The protagonist of James Weldon Johnson's *The Autobiography of an*

---

23. Hughes, *Not Without Laughter*, Ch. 7, pp. 77–80.
24. Scott, *Hurt, Baby, Hurt*, pp. 158–159.
25. John A. Williams, *This Is My Country Too* (New York: The New American Library, Inc., 1965), p. 127.
26. Du Bois, *The Souls of Black Folk*, p. 3.

Ex-Coloured Man echoes these sentiments at about the same time: "And this is the dwarfing, warping, distorting influence which operates upon each and every coloured man in the United States. He is forced to take his outlook on all things, not from the view-point of a citizen, or a man, or even a human being, but from the view-point of a *coloured* man."[27]

Nearly fifty years later John Howard Griffin found that the Negro was still allowed to see himself only through the eyes of others, and those eyes were often unseeing. The unseeing eyes, Griffin suggests, are even worse than the eyes that can see only the stereotype:

> The whites, especially the tourists, had no reticence before us, and no shame since we were Negroes. Some wanted to know where they could find girls, wanted us to get Negro girls for them. . . .
>
> Though not all, by any means, were so open about their purposes, all of them showed us how they felt about the Negro, the idea that we were people of such low morality that nothing could offend us.[28] These men, young and old, however, were less offensive than the ones who treated us like machines, as though we had no human existence whatsoever. When they paid me, they looked as though I were a stone or a post. They looked and saw nothing.[29]

Examples of the stereotypes in terms of which the Negro is forced to view himself may be seen in almost any one of these books. They range from fairly crude to fairly refined ones (if any stereotype may be called refined). Something of that range is suggested in these two passages from *Black Boy.* In the first one Wright describes his experience with a brutal family in whose store he worked:

> Each day in the store I watched the brutality with growing hate, yet trying to keep my feelings from registering in my face. When the boss looked at me I would avoid his eyes. Finally the boss's son cornered me one morning.
>
> "Say, nigger, look here," he began.
>
> "Yes, sir."

27. James Weldon Johnson, *The Autobiography of an Ex-Coloured Man* (Boston: Sherman, French and Company, 1912), Ch. 2, p. 19.
28. In this connection students will probably also have noticed the section on pp. 90–95 ("November 19") in which Griffin describes the "glow of prurience" with which whites asked him about Negro sexual practices.
29. John Howard Griffin, *Black Like Me* (Boston: Houghton Mifflin Company, 1961), "November 8," p. 28. Griffin is working as a shoeshine boy at this point in his trip.

"What's on your mind?"

"Nothing, sir," I said, trying to look amazed, trying to fool him.

"Why don't you laugh and talk like the other niggers?" he asked.

"Well, sir, there's nothing much to say or smile about," I said, smiling.

His face was hard, baffled; I knew that I had not convinced him. He whirled from me and went to the front of the store; he came back a moment later, his face red. He tossed a few green bills at me.

"I don't like your looks, nigger. Now, get!" he snapped.

I picked up the money and did not count it. I grabbed my hat and left.[30]

In the second passage Wright suggests the ways in which the white stereotypes have also affected the way in which the Negro sees himself:

I began to marvel at how smoothly the black boys acted out the roles that the white race had mapped out for them. Most of them were not conscious of living a special, separate, stunted way of life. Yet I knew that in some period of their growing up—a period that they had no doubt forgotten—there had been developed in them a delicate, sensitive controlling mechanism that shut off their minds and emotions from all that the white race had said was taboo. Although they lived in an America where in theory there existed equality of opportunity, they knew unerringly what to aspire to and what not to aspire to. Had a black boy announced that he aspired to be a writer, he would have been unhesitatingly called crazy by his pals. Or had a black boy spoken of yearning to get a seat on the New York Stock Exchange, his friends—in the boy's own interest—would have reported his odd ambition to the white boss.[31]

Students may point to a similar passage in *Manchild in the Promised Land*. Brown is describing the stereotyped role that his mother has accepted as appropriate for her race: "I could sense the fear in Mama's voice when I told her once that I wanted to be a psychologist. She said, 'Boy, you better stop that dreamin' and get all those crazy notions outta your head.' She was scared. She had the idea that

30. Wright, *Black Boy*, Ch. 9, pp. 159–160.
31. *Ibid.*, Ch. 10, p. 172.

colored people weren't supposed to want anything like that. You were supposed to just want to work in fields or be happy to be a janitor."[32]

Whereas the results of the first kind of cruelty—fear, hatred, subservience, defiance—are fairly simple, the results of the second kind of cruelty are much more complex. Psychologically, they produce the feeling which Ellison characterizes as "invisibility," and which Selina, the heroine of Paule Marshall's *Brown Girl, Brownstones*, describes in this way: "'The funny feeling you get is that they don't really see you. It's very eerie and infuriating. For a moment there until everybody suddenly got friendly I felt like I didn't exist but was only the projection of someone or something else in their mind's eye.'"[33] Selina, like Ellison's hero and like Wright, feels the desperate need to establish her own identity.[34] And the indirect cruelty of the stereotype often produces despair and takes away all hope from the Negro parent, who knows, as Griffin says, that "his children's lives would . . . be restricted, their world smaller, their educational opportunities less, their future mutilated." This is, Griffin believes, "the least obvious but most heinous of all race crimes, for it kills the spirit and the will to live."[35] Langston Hughes' hero, Sandy, feels some of this desperation. He realizes that some white people "are pretty decent," but at the same time recognizes that they have prevented "advancement for colored fellows." If Negroes "start as porters, they stay porters for ever and they can't come up. Being colored is like being born in the basement of life, with the door to the light locked and barred—and the white folks live upstairs. They don't want us up there with them, even when we're respectable like Dr. Mitchell, or smart like Dr. Du Bois."[36] Frank Yerby's protagonist in *Speak Now* feels that "being black is . . . a species of death by inches, daily. When it isn't something worse: the annihilation of personality. . . ."[37]

But perhaps an even more pernicious effect of white stereotypes, as Griffin points out, is the Negro's discrimination against himself: "Walking . . . through the ghetto, I realized that every informed man with whom I had spoken, in the intimate freedom of the colored bond, had acknowledged a double problem for the Negro. First, the discrimination against him. Second, and almost more grievous, his discrimination against himself; his contempt for the blackness that he

---

32. Brown, *Manchild in the Promised Land,* Ch. 11, p. 281. Students might also note the passage in Ch. 3 (p. 75) in which Brown himself immediately assumes that a black school official will have no power to help him.
33. Paule Marshall, *Brown Girl, Brownstones* (New York: Random House, Inc., 1959), Bk. 4, Ch. 6, p. 253.
34. Compare Wright, *Black Boy,* Ch. 14, pp. 226–227.
35. Griffin, *Black Like Me,* "November 24," p. 120.
36. Hughes, *Not Without Laughter,* Ch. 26, pp. 280–281.
37. Frank Yerby, *Speak Now* (New York: Dial Press, Inc., 1969), Ch. 4, p. 75.

associates with his suffering; his willingness to sabotage his fellow Negroes because they are part of the blackness he has found so painful."[38]

This attitude is reflected in Brown's account of his father's reference to one of Brown's darkest friends as "that black so-and-so," and his reference to Brown's light-skinned friends as "nice" or "nice-lookin'."[39] It is reflected in the delight of Langston Hughes' protagonist's sister that in the church she belongs to there is "never anything niggerish" about the services, and in her acceptance as a compliment of this remark from her employer: "'You're so smart and such a good, clean, quick little worker, Tempy, that it's too bad you aren't white.'"[40] Zora Neale Hurston describes the same phenomenon in her character Mrs. Turner, who believes that "anyone who looked more white folkish than herself was better than she was in her criteria, therefore it was right that they should be cruel to her at times, just as she was cruel to those more negroid than herself in direct ratio to their negroness. Like the pecking-order in a chicken yard. Insensate cruelty to those you can whip, and grovelling submission to those you can't."[41] Wallace Thurman castigates the same attitude in *The Blacker the Berry:* "There was nothing quite so silly as the creed of the blue veins: 'Whiter and whiter, every generation. The nearer white you are the more white people will respect you. Therefore all light Negroes marry light Negroes. Continue to do so generation after generation, and eventually white people will accept this racially bastard aristocracy, thus enabling those Negroes who really matter to escape the social and economic inferiority of the American Negro.'"[42] Later in the novel one of the characters explains how the attitude has come about:

> "As I was saying," Truman continued, "you can't blame light Negroes for being prejudiced against dark ones. All of you know that white is the symbol of everything pure and good, whether that everything be concrete or abstract. Ivory Soap is advertised as being ninety-nine and some fraction per cent pure, and Ivory Soap is white. Moreover, virtue and virginity are always represented as being clothed in white garments. Then, too, the God we, or rather most Negroes worship is a patriarchal white man, seated on a white throne, in a spotless white Heaven, radiant with

38. Griffin, *Black Like Me,* "November 10–12," p. 44.
39. Brown, *Manchild in the Promised Land,* Ch. 11, p. 276.
40. Hughes, *Not Without Laughter,* Ch. 13, 23; pp. 165, 254.
41. Zora Neale Hurston, *Their Eyes Were Watching God* (New York: J. B. Lippincott Company, 1937), Ch. 16, p. 215.
42. Wallace Thurman, *The Blacker the Berry* (New York: Macaulay Company, 1929), Part 1, p. 29.

white streets and white-apparelled angels eating white honey and drinking white milk. . . ."

"We are all living in a totally white world, where all standards are standards of the white man, and where almost invariably what the white man does is right, and what the black man does is wrong, unless it is precedented by something a white man has done."

"Which," Cora added scornfully, "makes it all right for light Negroes to discriminate against dark ones?"

"Not at all," Truman objected. "It merely explains, not justifies the evil."[43]

It is also the insistence of whites on stereotypes and the resulting inability of blacks to see themselves except through the eyes of others that has sometimes contributed to the rigidity and the injustice of what might be termed the "Black Establishment." One sees this in the way that Bledsoe treats the hero of *Invisible Man*, banishing him from school and blighting his chances of securing a job simply because he has had the ill fortune to expose the white benefactor of the school to some of the realities of Negro life. This can be seen also in *Black Boy* in the principal's refusal to let Wright deliver his own graduation speech and his insistence that he deliver the speech which the principal has written.

Another question that students might be asked is: What effect has the treatment of blacks in America had upon whites? Students might point to examples, particularly noteworthy in Baldwin's *The Fire Next Time* and Brown's *Manchild in the Promised Land,* in which the moral dilemma of whites is pointed out. Baldwin speaks of the "very strange ring" that the terms "civilized" and "Christian" have in the light of recent history and particularly of Nazi atrocities;[44] and Brown, reporting a conversation with his friend Floyd Saks, underscores the fact that Christianity has not led the white man to help the Negro:

This Christianity thing is the worst thing that ever happened to Negroes. If it wasn't for Christianity, Negroes would have stopped praying a long time ago. They would've started raising a whole lot of hell. They would've known. There would've been thousands of Nat Turners and Denmark Veseys. But most of the Negroes were too damn busy looking up in the sky and praying to some blond-haired, blue-eyed Jesus and some white God who

43. *Ibid.,* Part 4, pp. 165–166.
44. Baldwin, *The Fire Next Time,* "Down at the Cross," p. 66.

nobody was suppose to ever see or know anything about. You look at it around here. The Negro's got a whole lot of religion, the so-called Negro, the black man. He's got more religion than anything else.

But he's till poor; he's still being abused. So why the hell don't the white man take some of that religion he's been preaching to us all the time and give us some of the money? Why don't he take some of that religion and use it himself, to make himself less mean and stop killing all those people, lynching all those people down there in Georgia, Mississippi, and Alabama? If there was anything to this white man's religion, he wouldn't be so damn wicked. How can he be so righteous, how can the religion that he's living by be so righteous, if it's going to let him come in here and take a whole country from the Indians, kill off most of them, and put the remainder of them on reservations?[45]

As the latter part of this passage suggests, black Americans have begun to make America aware of a wider set of inconsistencies in American history. Baldwin explains this:

The American Negro has the great advantage of having never believed that collection of myths to which white Americans cling: that their ancestors were all freedom-loving heroes, that they were born in the greatest country the world has ever seen, or that Americans are invincible in battle and wise in peace, that Americans have always dealt honorably with Mexicans and Indians and all other neighbors or inferiors, that American men are the world's most direct and virile, that American women are pure. Negroes know far more about white Americans than that; it can almost be said, in fact, that they know about white Americans what parents—or, anyway, mothers—know about their children, and that they very often regard white Americans that way. And perhaps this attitude, held in spite of what they know and have endured, helps to explain why Negroes, on the whole, and until lately, have allowed themselves to feel so little hatred. The tendency has really been, insofar as this was possible, to dismiss white people as the slightly mad victims of their own brainwashing.[46]

Eldridge Cleaver makes the same point, suggesting that the younger generation of whites is beginning to reject some of the myths of the

45. Brown, *Manchild in the Promised Land,* Ch. 14, pp. 320–321.
46. Baldwin, *The Fire Next Time,* "Down at the Cross," pp. 115–116.

older generation, and hence that in present-day America the gap between generations may be more extensive than the gap between races:

> It is among the white youth of the world that the greatest change is taking place. It is they who are experiencing the great psychic pain of waking into consciousness to find their inherited heroes turned by events into villains. Communication and understanding between the older and younger generations of whites has entered a crisis. The elders, who, in the tradition of privileged classes or races, genuinely do not understand the youth, trapped by old ways of thinking and blind to the future, have only just begun to be vexed—because the youth have only just begun to rebel. So thoroughgoing is the revolution in the psyches of white youth that the traditional tolerance which every older generation has found it necessary to display is quickly exhausted, leaving a gulf of fear, hostility, mutual misunderstanding, and contempt.[47]

Griffin, writing about his friend, white Southern journalist P. D. East, states the philosophical principle at the center of the contradictions that white America has indulged in:

> [East] continued stubbornly to preach justice. He said that in order to prove that the Negroes have no right to their freedoms, we are subverting the very principles that preserve the spirit of our own . . . we are endangering ourselves, no matter what our race and creed.
>
> In essence, he asked for ethical and virtuous social conduct. He said that before we can have justice, we must first have truth, and he insisted on his right and duty to print the truth. Significantly, this was considered high treason.[48]

Griffin also shows a more immediate and dangerous effect of prejudice on whites in describing an incident when he had been picked up and given a ride at night by a white man. The conversation takes an ugly turn as the man describes how he has taken sexual advantage of his Negro employees and Griffin has been unable, even in silence, to hide his disapproval. The man asks whether Griffin has come to stir up trouble and then threatens him:

---

47. Eldridge Cleaver, *Soul on Ice* (New York: McGraw-Hill Book Company, 1968), Part 2, "The White Race and Its Heroes," pp. 69–70.
48. Griffin, *Black Like Me*, "November 14," p. 78.

"Do you know what we do to troublemakers down here?"

"No sir."

"We either ship them off to the pen or kill them."

He spoke in a tone that sickened me, casual, merciless. I looked at him. His decent blue eyes turned yellow. I knew that nothing could touch him to have mercy once he decided a Negro should be "taught a lesson." The immensity of it terrified me. But it caught him up like a lust now. He entertained it, his voice unctuous with pleasure and cruelty. The highway stretched deserted through the swamp forests. He nodded toward the solid wall of brush flying past our windows.

"You can kill a nigger and toss him into that swamp and no one'll ever know what happened to him."

"Yes sir . . ."

I forced myself to silence, forced myself to picture this man in his other roles. I saw him as he played with his grandchildren, as he stood up in church with open hymnal in hand, as he drank a cup of coffee in the morning before dressing and then shaved and talked with his wife pleasantly about nothing, as he visited with friends on the front porch Sunday afternoons. That was the man I had seen when I first got into the truck. The amiable, decent American was in all his features. This was the dark tangent in every man's belly, the sickness, the coldness, the mercilessness, the lust to cause pain or fear through self-power. Surely not even his wife or closest friends had ever seen him like this. It was a side he would show no one but his victims, or those who connived with him. The rest—what he really must be as a husband, devoted father and respected member of the community—I had to supply with my imagination. He showed me the lowest and I had to surmise the highest.[49]

Langston Hughes likewise suggests the destructiveness of hate and the necessity for love in *Not Without Laughter*. Hager is talking to her grandson, Sandy:

"I's been livin' a long time in yesterday, Sandy chile, an' I knows there ain't no room in de world fo' nothin' mo'n love. I knows, chile! Ever'thing there is but lovin' leaves a rust on yo' soul. An' to love sho 'nough, you got to have a spot in yo' heart fo' ever'body—great an' small, white an' black, an' them what's good an' them what's evil—'cause love ain't got no crowded-out

49. *Ibid.*, "November 24," pp. 110–111.

places where de good ones stays an' de bad ones can't come in. When it gets that way, then it ain't love.

"White peoples maybe mistreats you 'n hates you, but when you hates 'em back, you's de one what's hurted, 'cause hate makes yo' heart ugly—that's all it does. It closes up de sweet door to life an' makes ever'thing small an' mean an' dirty. Honey, there ain't no room in de world fo' hate, white folks hatin' niggers, an' niggers hatin' white folks. There ain't no room in this world fo' nothin' but love, Sandy chile. That's all they's room fo'—nothin' but love."[50]

Baldwin states the general principle involved here, as he warns Negroes against retaliating in kind to white cruelty:

I am very much concerned that American Negroes achieve their freedom here in the United States. But I am also concerned for their dignity, for the health of their souls, and must oppose any attempt that Negroes may make to do to others what has been done to them. I think I know—we see it around us every day—the spiritual wasteland to which that road leads. It is so simple a fact and one that is so hard, apparently, to grasp: *Whoever debases others is debasing himself.* That is not a mystical statement but a most realistic one, which is proved by the eyes of any Alabama sheriff—and I would not like to see Negroes ever arrive at so wretched a condition.[51]

Studying these passages, students will come to see that the problem is as much a white as a black one: "Whoever debases others is debasing himself." Thus it is that Baldwin asserts that "if the word *integration* means anything, this is what it means: that we, with love, shall force our brothers to see themselves as they are, to cease fleeing from reality and begin to change it."[52]

This definition of integration may well be different from the one that students have, since they may have assumed that integration simply means giving Negroes the opportunity to mix with whites. But the situation is more complicated. As Baldwin says, "White Americans find it as difficult as white people elsewhere do to divest themselves of the notion that they are in possession of some intrinsic value that black people need, or want." And when the Negro succeeds, "It is the Negro, of course, who is presumed to have become

50. Hughes, *Not Without Laughter*, Ch. 16, p. 194. Cf. Griffin, *Black Like Me*, "November 19," pp. 103–104.
51. Baldwin, *The Fire Next Time*, "Down at the Cross," p. 97.
52. *Ibid.*, "My Dungeon Shook," pp. 23–24.

equal—an achievement that not only proves the comforting fact that perseverance has no color but also overwhelmingly corroborates the white man's sense of his own value."[53] Thus, although some blacks have felt that the best answer to black problems lies in achieving better educational opportunities for blacks, Baldwin feels that "there is simply no possibility of a real change in the Negro's situation without the most radical and far-reaching changes in the American political and social structure. And it is clear," he continues, "that white Americans are not simply unwilling to effect these changes; they are, in the main, so slothful have they become, unable even to envision them."[54]

During recent years there have been at least four groups, holding competing philosophies, among those proposing solutions for the problems of the Negro: those who advocate working for better educational opportunities and gradual change, those who favor a more militant approach to integration, those who favor separatism or black nationalism, and those who feel as Baldwin does, that Negro problems are part of a much larger context and that the whole society must be restructured.

But there is another way to classify solutions to the problems of the Negro, one which is more closely tied to students' appreciation of the literary qualities and universal elements of these books. Throughout history men have sought solutions to their problems either as individuals or as members of a group—that is, through the efforts of the individual man or woman or through organized activity. In the case of the Negro, organized activity, stemming from the philosophies described above, has had, depending upon the organization, at least three different purposes. First of all, there is the civil rights movement, the goal of which is to achieve civil rights and integration for Negroes. More recently, there have been the black nationalist movements which have concentrated on achieving power for the Negro for separatist goals. Thirdly, there are the groups that are attempting to bring changes throughout the society as a whole by attacking both the black and the white establishments. The activities of these organizations can be traced through historical sources of one kind or another, and further material for discussion about these organizations may be found in many of the works we have been considering.

More purely literary sources, however, will give students a better look at the actions of individuals who have achieved individual solutions of one sort or another. Brown's book, for example, is a kind of declaration of independence. First of all, he refuses to treat whites stereotypically, as in this description of his defense of a white boy

53. *Ibid.*, "Down at the Cross," pp. 108–109.
54. *Ibid.*, "Down at the Cross," p. 99.

whom other black boys were mistreating: "There was no white, no color thing. To me, he was a beautiful cat; and if you dug people and if people had something that was beautiful about them, they were raceless."[55] Secondly, he accepts sole responsibility for his own fate and tells a story which he heard and will "always remember," illustrating the importance of individual persistence:

> There were two frogs sitting on a milk vat one time. The frogs fell into the milk vat. It was very deep. They kept swimming and swimming around, and they couldn't get out. They couldn't climb out because they were too far down. One frog said, "Oh, I can't make it, and I'm going to give up." And the other frog kept swimming and swimming. His arms became more and more tired, and it was harder and harder and harder for him to swim. Then he couldn't do another stroke. He couldn't throw one more arm into the milk. He kept trying and trying; it seemed as if the milk was getting hard and heavy. He kept trying; he knows that he's going to die, but as long as he's got this little bit of life in him, he's going to keep on swimming. On his last stroke, it seemed as though he had to pull a whole ocean back, but he did it and found himself sitting on top of a vat of butter.[56]

This little parable should provide material for lively discussion, as students explore such questions as how the frogs got in the milk vat in the first place, what happens if one frog is too weak to keep swimming until the butter is formed, and whether the milk vat should be eliminated because it is hazardous to frogs.

Tucker Caliban in William Kelley's *A Different Drummer* displays a similar kind of independence: an organizer from a "Society" devoted to helping Negroes secure their rights has solicited Tucker to become a member. Tucker replies:

> "They ain't working for my rights. Ain't nobody working for my rights; I wouldn't let them."
>
> The Society-person said that whether or not Tucker let them, they were doing it anyway, that the decisions they won in the courts would help his children go to school and get a good education.
>
> "So what?" That was Tucker's answer. "So what?" he said in that high, chirpy voice like an old man's. . . .
>
> "Well, whether you like it or not, the Society is fighting your battles in the courts and you should support them."

55. Brown, *Manchild in the Promised Land,* Ch. 4, p. 132.
56. *Ibid.,* Ch. 4, p. 123.

Tucker just sat there. "Ain't none of my battles being fought in no courts. I'm fighting all my battles myself."

"You can't fight all this alone. What battles?"

"My very own battles . . . all mine, and either I beat them or they beat me. And ain't no piece of cardboard [i.e. membership card] making no difference in how it turns out."[57]

A little later in the novel Reverend Bradshaw, a leader in the movement for civil rights, comments to the narrator on attitudes like Tucker's:

"You spoke of the Tuckers not needing you, not needing their leaders. Did you ever think that a person like myself, a so-called religious leader needs the Tuckers to justify his existence? The day is fast coming, Mister Willson, when people will realize there isn't any need for me and people like me. Perhaps for me that day has come already. Your Tuckers will get up and say: I can do anything I want; I don't need to wait for someone to GIVE me freedom; I can take it myself. I don't need Mister Leader, Mister Boss, Mister President, Mister Priest, or Mister Minister, or Reverend Bradshaw. I don't need anyone. I can do whatever I want for myself by myself."[58]

Bradshaw perceives this sadly: he realizes that he has become "obsolete," since people like Tucker can act as individuals to achieve their goals without the help of leaders and organizations. This passage might lead to a further discussion of whether organizations are ever obsolete in society, whether societies ever reach the point where individuals can achieve for themselves all that they need to achieve.

This is a universal question and there are many other universal elements in these books that go beyond the immediate theme of the black experience. To cite but one example, there is the passage in *Beetlecreek* describing the suffocating effect of the town of Beetlecreek upon David, Johnny's uncle:

Sitting in the corner against the white wall of the church, he thought of being trapped in the village, arrested, closed in.

Often he would sit on the railing of the swinging bridge, looking down at the creek, watching the current. He would watch floating things—boxes, tin cans, bottles. He would watch how some of these things became trapped in the reeds alongside the

57. William Melvin Kelley, *A Different Drummer* (New York: Doubleday & Company, Inc., 1962), "Dymphna Willson," p. 120.
58. *Ibid.*, "Dewey Willson, III," p. 145.

shore. First there was a whirlpool to entice the floating object, then a slow-flowing pool, and finally, the deadly mud backwater in the reeds. In the reeds would be other objects already trapped. This was Beetlecreek, he thought. And he knew that, like the rusty cans, he was trapped, caught, unable to move again.

This was like when he first became aware of being suffocated—the suffocation he had felt in church, the undercurrent of secret excitement he knew they felt partaking of the death ritual, the secret envy for the escape death offered, the jealousy of the escaped one; the hunger to be joined together in something, anything, even the celebration of death; the secret meanings communicated seated before the corpse; the feast; the singing; the sermon; the joviality of the handshakes on the porch steps; the admiration of Baily Brothers' shiny new hearse; the terrible importance of Death to lives that had little importance; the justification of life in death. He too had felt all these things, knowing at the same time that his feeling for the girl had meaning only because it brought movement to his life (a life which had become static, caught in the creek reeds, turned rusty and muddy), had importance because it lifted the suffocation from him.[59]

This is an excellent description of the deadening effect that any town might have upon its citizens, black or white, though David happens to be black. These townspeople are kinsmen to Thoreau's "mass of men" who "lead lives of quiet desperation."[60] A very different, yet no less universal view of a town is to be found in the picture of Cherokee Flats that Gordon Parks presents in *The Learning Tree*. Newt Winger has asked his mother, Sarah, whether they are going to live all their life in the town:

Sarah looked searchingly at him. "Don't you like it here?"

"I don't know, Momma. I ain't never been no place else."

"I hope you won't have to stay here all your life, Newt. It ain't a all-good place and it ain't a all-bad place. But you can learn just as much here about people and things as you can learn any place else. Cherokee Flats is sorta like a fruit tree. Some of the people are good and some of them are bad—just like the fruit on a tree. You know that, don't you, boy?"

"Yessem."

"Well, if you learn to profit from the good and bad these people

59. William Demby, *Beetlecreek* (New York: Holt, Rinehart & Winston, Inc., 1950), Part 3, Ch. 2, pp. 93–94.
60. See pp. 76–77 above for further remarks on this passage from Thoreau.

do to each other, you'll learn a lot 'bout life. And you'll be a better man for that learnin' someday. Understand?"

"Yessem."

"No matter if you go or stay, think of Cherokee Flats like that till the day you die—let it be your learnin' tree."[61]

Beetlecreek, Cherokee Flats, Concord, Our Town, Hannibal, Missouri—each tells something important about America.

Summary

What should students take away from this unit? First of all, surely, a better understanding of what it has meant to be black in America: an understanding of what it can mean to live under cruelty and fear, an understanding of what it means to struggle against despair, and an understanding of how difficult it may be to be one's self in defiance of a stereotype. Tempe, in Langston Hughes' *Not Without Laughter*, "got her recipes from *The Ladies' Home Journal*—and she never bought a watermelon,"[62] while Ralph Ellison's protagonist in *Invisible Man* had to struggle not to feel "ashamed of the things I had always loved," before buying the baked yams from the street vendor. "What and how much had I lost by trying to do only what was expected of me instead of what I myself had wished to do? What a waste, what a senseless waste!" he concludes.[63] Banjo, the central character in Claude McKay's novel, makes a similar declaration about his instrument:

"Banjo! That's what you play?" exclaimed Goosey.

"Sure that's what I play," replied Banjo. "Don't you like it?"

"No. Banjo is bondage. It's the instrument of slavery. Banjo is Dixie. The Dixie of the land of cotton and massa and missus and black mammy. We colored folks have got to get away from all that in these enlightened progressive days. Let us play piano and violin, harp and flute. Let the white folks play the banjo if they want to keep on remembering all the Black Joes singing and the hell they made them live in."

"That ain't got nothing to do with me, nigger," replied Banjo. "I play that theah instrument becaz I likes it."[64]

---

61. Gordon Parks, *The Learning Tree* (New York: Harper & Row, Publishers, 1963), Ch. 2, pp. 37–38.
62. Hughes, *Not Without Laughter*, Ch. 23, p. 254.
63. Ralph Ellison, *Invisible Man* (New York: Random House, Inc., 1947), Ch. 13, pp. 199–202.
64. Claude McKay, *Banjo* (New York: Harper & Row, Publishers, 1929), Ch. 7, p. 90.

And, for many of these protagonists, being one's self means not only conquering fear of the stereotype but conquering hate as well. Solly, the hero of John Oliver Killens' *And Then We Heard the Thunder*, comes to this realization as he reads Richard Wright's *Twelve Million Black Voices* while he is in the hospital:

> One day he was reading the book and it suddenly came to him, and he said to himself, if I'm proud of me, I don't need to hate Mister Charlie's people. I don't want to. I don't need to. If I love me, I can also love the whole damn human race. Black, brown, yellow, white. . . . He looked around at the other soldiers in his ward, most of them white, and he loved the whole damn miserable wonderful human race.[65]

More important, students should come away from this unit with a recognition of the complexity of the problems that an examination of the black experience suggests. They should have a greater awareness of the many, often subtle ways in which the problems are white problems as well as black problems. But, most important, they should also have a sense of the power of literature to present the black experience as a reflection of universal experience. As Clive tells Selina in Paule Marshall's *Brown Girl, Brownstones,* one must not accept the handicap of a stereotype, must not

> "admit what some white people would have you admit and what some Negroes do admit—that you are only Negro, some flat, one-dimensional, bas-relief figure which is supposed to explain everything about you. You commit an injustice against yourself by admitting that, because, first, you rule out your humanity, and second, your complexity as a human being. Oh hell, I'm not saying that being black in this goddamn white world isn't crucial. No one but us knows how corrosive it is, how it maims us all, how it rings our lives. But at some point you have to break through to the larger ring which encompasses us all—our humanity. To understand that much about us can be simply explained by the fact that we're men, caught with all men within the common ring."[66]

In other words, if the teacher has been successful, students will come away from this unit with the conviction that their horizons have been broadened and that they have added something significant to their knowledge about the human condition.

65. John Oliver Killens, *And Then We Heard the Thunder* (New York: Alfred A. Knopf, Inc., 1963), Part 4, Ch. 1, p. 362.
66. Marshall, *Brown Girl, Brownstones*, Bk. 4, Ch. 6, p. 252.

PART FIVE

Three Novelists Speak

In the following pages, three novelists comment on their own work and on the writing and teaching of fiction. They come from diverse backgrounds and have written different kinds of books. Conrad Richter was drawn to the American past and particularly to the days when white man and Indian came into conflict on the frontier. Alan Paton has written of the present-day conflicts in his native South Africa between black natives and white colonists of European descent. John Knowles finds conflict in another setting in his most famous novel, *A Separate Peace,* which tells the story of the rivalry of boys at an Eastern American prep school against the background of the larger struggle of World War ii. No critic would make the mistake of saying that these three novelists belonged to the same school or wrote the same kind of books.

Yet the three authors are in agreement on a surprising number of ideas, and their agreement has implications for the teaching of fiction. All three think of themselves primarily as "story tellers" and wish for readers who will read their books first and foremost for the story. "My own firm belief," says Alan Paton, "is that a writer must, above all, tell a story." Conrad Richter says, "I know of no way at the moment to instill a love of reading in a child except by telling him a story that greatly interests him." And John Knowles agrees: "I think a novel should be taken at face value first—as an experience." This means, Knowles continues, concentrating first on "a very special concrete set of people and experiences," and then, if one wishes, going on "into the underlying reverberations and themes as secondary values." Implications for the teacher are clear: he should not hurry to get to the theme of a book; he should let a class come to an understanding of the thematic dimension of a book only after they have experienced and enjoyed the "very special concrete set of people and experiences."

At the same time, all three writers are in agreement that the other sides of a novel—its "informational" side, as Knowles puts it, or its "controversial" side, as Paton says—are not to be neglected. Richter says he tried to give "each side its due" in his treatment of the Indians and the white men, and he found that the ending of *The Light in the Forest* had "value in mildly shocking the reader and making him question and think." Again, the implications for the teacher are clear: students can enjoy and profit from the "informational" side of some novels— "the picture of Dickens' London," for example—even though, as Knowles says, this "journalistic or sociological" role of the novel has been taken over in part by newspapers, magazines, and television. More important, the student, like any other reader, should be led, in Richter's words, to "question and think." If the questioning and thinking come out of a previous discussion and understanding of the people and events of the story, then discussions of theme have a solid base from which to proceed; they can safely range back and forth between the book and the general thematic issue without the danger of leaving the book behind in a bull session on a controversial topic merely suggested by the book. As Paton says, neither the topical nor the universal should be stressed exclusively, for "these two things are inseparable."

All three writers also agree that the same work of fiction can legitimately be read in different ways by readers of differing literary sophistication. Though Knowles thinks that very young readers could not understand *A Separate Peace,* he feels that ninth graders can get something from the book, adding only that he hopes they will go back and read it again at twenty-one or twenty-five when they can get even more. Paton agrees that "some novels can be successfully taught at different levels in different ways"; he puts his own *Cry, the Beloved Country* in that group, instancing appreciative letters he has received from writers "whose ages vary from fourteen to eighty." Richter believes that "all novels . . . can be reduced to a simple theme and purpose academically." The most important goal of the teacher is that students be "taught and infected with an intimate interest in and understanding of the characters and story, together with some appreciation of the art of good writing." Paton reinforces this idea: for him, getting "pupils to grow excited over the use of words and the use of language" is the most important goal for a teacher, since "this infection with enthusiasm is the most important experience that a student can have."

Knowles says that "writing a novel is like peeling an onion, reaching successive layers of significance." Perhaps teaching a novel is the same; one starts with the "very special concrete set of people and experiences" and then goes on to the "underlying reverberations"—the questioning and thinking about controversial thematic issues—all the time noticing the excitement created by the language of the book itself.

CONRAD RICHTER

Photo: Alfred A. Knopf, Inc.

Conrad Richter was born October 13, 1890, in Pine Grove, Pennsylvania. As a young boy, he later reported, he "tried to run away to the West and fight Indians." After attending the public schools he started to work at fifteen "in the Vulcan depths of a . . . machine shop." Over the course of the next few years he held such various jobs as teamster, farm hand, bank teller, timberman, and subscription salesman. At nineteen he turned to a newspaper career and soon began writing for magazines in his spare time. While living on a farm between 1922 and 1928 he continued to publish short stories.

He moved to New Mexico with his family in 1928, where he was able to collect material on early American life which was later to find its way into his fiction. Richter's first novel, *The Sea of Grass* (Alfred A. Knopf, Inc., 1937) was followed by a succession of other novels, some of them dealing with the Southwest, including *Tacey Cromwell* (Knopf, 1942) and *The Lady* (Knopf, 1957). His Ohio historical trilogy, *The Trees, The Fields,* and *The Town,* was published by Knopf between 1940 and 1950. *The Light in the Forest,* which was published by Knopf in 1953, almost immediately won its way into many junior and senior high school curriculums. During the sixties his novels included *The Waters of Kronos, A Simple Honorable Man,* and *The Grandfathers* (Knopf, 1960, 1962, 1964, respectively).

Among the honors Richter received were the Gold Medal for Literature of the Society of Libraries of New York University for *The Sea of Grass* and *The Trees* (1942), the Ohioana Library Medal (1947), the Pulitzer Prize in fiction for *The Town* (1951), a National Institute of Arts and Letters grant in literature (1959), the Maggie Award for *The Lady* (1959), and the National Book Award for *The Waters of Kronos* (1961). He held honorary degrees from Susquehanna University and the University of New Mexico.

Richter married Harvena M. Achenbach in 1915; their daughter Harvena Richter has followed in her father's footsteps to write fiction, nonfiction, and poetry. The Richters returned from New Mexico to settle permanently in Pine Grove in 1950. Mr. Richter died in the fall of 1968. Answers to the questions from which this interview was constructed were the last thing he worked on before his death.

An Interview with Conrad Richter

Q. Mr. Richter, one of the most important goals of the English teacher is to create willing and enthusiastic readers among his students. You once said in a radio broadcast:

> All my life I have been a reader, and one of my joys, especially as a boy and young man, was to come on a book in which I could lose myself. If at such a time someone spoke to me, I might not hear him. If he touched me, I would come reluctantly out of my book as from another world. All the while I listened to the interrupter or went about the task he or she had given me, the world of my book would hang luminous and inviting behind me, waiting like a live and teeming dream into which I might return as soon as my task was done.[1]

English teachers would be happy if they could produce readers of this kind. Do you think a love of books like this can be taught? Did your own schooling play any part in developing your love of reading?

A. I suspect that, by and large, readers are born and not made, although the parents or teacher and perhaps an environment to escape from may help nourish and enrich the talent. My feeling is that educators cannot expect to be God, cannot take the place of ancestors and genes that have gone before. I know of no way at the moment to instill a love of reading in a child except by telling him a story that greatly interests him. In my own case I went to my great aunt's kindergarten, learned my letters early, read the Harry Castlemon and G.A. Henty books somewhere between six and eight. My great aunt was an inveterate story teller, which may have helped, although it didn't seem to help some of my school mates. My feeling that I didn't belong in my environment may have helped also. But the love of reading was there, perhaps from my mother's side. She loved Scott; her sister, Dickens. Their uncles were editors.

This "interview" is based on written responses that Mr. Richter made to a number of questions in late October 1968, just before his final illness. It was my arrangement with him that these responses would be edited and rearranged to form an interview, subject to his final approval. His daughter, critic and novelist Harvena Richter, has been kind enough to approve this final form for the interview, in which none of Mr. Richter's words have been altered, although the responses have been rearranged and there have been a few deletions from the original responses.
1. "Far Away and Long Ago," quoted in Edwin W. Gaston, Jr., *Conrad Richter* (New York: Twayne Publishers, Inc., 1965), p. 27.

Q. I would infer from this love of reading that writing came naturally to you. What have been the main influences upon your work and especially upon *The Light in the Forest,* a book which is read each school year by many high school and junior high school classes? Are there incidents from your own experience?

A. As a young boy I tried to run away to the West and fight Indians, but grown older and wiser, I hope, "I put away childish things."

Q. What drew your interest to the frontier, the setting for many of your stories?

A. When I came to New Mexico in the 1920s, many men and women who had lived through the frontier era were still living. Some of them became my warm friends and gave me firsthand pictures of their experiences that cried to be told. This led to later interest in the Eastern frontier, stories of which were told me as a boy. We were living at 7,200 feet in the mountains of New Mexico when a neighbor gave me Henry Howe's *Historical Collections of Ohio* to read. This immense reservoir of authentic early material absorbed me, and the idea of the Ohio trilogy was born at that time high up in the big pines of the Southwestern mountains.

Q. How do you translate historical raw material into fiction? What is the relationship between history and fiction?

A. I am not aware of the relationship between history and fiction but of a great deal between history and story. My ears were filled as a boy with early American stories and anecdotes. Except for two instances in *The Light in the Forest,* there is little actual identity of historical figures and places in my novels. This would be confining to theme, story and truth, although I notice it doesn't appear to bother some others who tell the reader what they imagine actual people said at a given place and time.

Q. How do you go about selecting material from your knowledge of history for inclusion in your stories?

A. My selection of material is a process in me of which I am not the creator but follow feelings and judgment. I should not care to analyze these. The faculty would probably become self-conscious, mechanical and be lost.

Q. Eudora Welty has commented that "the moment the place in which the novel happens is accepted as true, through it will begin to glow in a kind of recognizable glory the feeling and thought that inhabited the novel in the author's head and animated the whole of his work. . . . Location pertains to feeling, feeling profoundly pertains to Place; Place in history partakes of feeling, as feeling about history partakes of Place."² Does this in any way describe your own feeling and practice about the importance of setting in historical fiction?

A. Regarding Eudora Welty's quotation, a child may feel the most farfetched nonsense to be true and many undeveloped readers will avidly live stories that to me are no more real than abstractions drawn by a monkey's tail or automobile tires. I feel the historical setting has little part in authenticity, which is rather the province of the author's knowledge, honesty, and story-telling skill. However, the historical idea or implied analogies have considerable importance in the breadth and depth of theme and meaning.

Q. In the Preface to *The Light in the Forest* you spoke of one purpose or theme for that novel: "I thought that perhaps if we understood how these First Americans felt toward us even then and toward our white way of life, we might better understand the adverse, if perverted, view of us by some African, European, and Asian peoples today." Does historical fiction often have a similar relationship with the present?

A. Surely wise historical fiction should throw some light on present conditions.

Q. You also said in the Preface to *The Light in the Forest* that another part of your purpose was "to point out that in the pride of our American liberties, we're apt to forget that already we've lost a good many to civilization. The American Indians once enjoyed far more than we." What particular liberties were you thinking about and have they been completely lost?

A. Much of the old fierce pleasure in freedom and in the discipline of hardship and overcoming it has dissipated, but is still to be found in the young.

Q. You say in the Preface to *The Light in the Forest* that the novel doesn't represent your "particular beliefs or opinions" and that you could "understand and sympathize with either side," since it was your attempt "to be fair to them both." Yet I wonder if nearly all readers don't feel that the Indians are presented more sympathetically than the whites. Did you intend for your readers to take sides?

A. I receive hundreds of letters from readers, mostly students and their teachers. Of these, I recall only one rather sullen youngster who defended the whites and indicted the mass guilt of the Indians. The intelligent reader knows that all Indians were not

2. Eudora Welty, *Three Papers on Fiction* (Northampton, Mass.: Smith College, 1962), pp. 5–6.

noble and all whites ignoble, although he may not know that whites who took up with the Indians, signally a few of Scotch blood, often became more cruel and bloodthirsty than the savages themselves. The Paxton men, nearly all Scotch Presbyterians, did actually and historically murder in cold blood a settlement of Christian Indians in Lancaster County, mutilating women and children while still alive, this only one of many incidents of its kind. It is quite true that Indians did the same, but it was their normal means of war and they also had the benefit of a just cause, defense of their land and retaliation against its being taken over by white colonials who burned game cover, ploughed over Indian graves, and established themselves as owners. The action of the whites, on the other hand, derived from hate of those they had dispossessed. I have no wish to convert anyone. Those who believe that more enlightened peoples have the right to destroy the less enlightened and make more civilized use of their land will view the situation from their own sympathies along with those today who have willingly given up their birthright for gadgetry and ease.

Q.   Could the Indians in *The Light in the Forest* be called typical?

A.   In regard to Indians, it should be understood that tribes varied in cruelty and untrustworthiness. The novel in question concerns the Delawares who, despite what their wily enemies said about them, were the Romans of early Eastern America, their language a kind of Indian Latin which often formed the basis of communication between Indian nations. Much confusion has arisen from the assumption that the Indians of today are those of yesterday as found by the first Europeans on arriving here. Joaquin Miller eloquently tells of the great difference between early Indians he knew in California and their descendants.

Q.   Your short story "As It Was in the Beginning"[3] makes interesting parallel reading to *The Light in the Forest* with its contrasts in sympathy, point of view, and tone. Do you have any comments on the two works in the light of their differing origins or purposes?

A.   Yes, this is an example of giving each side its due. The Apaches, despite TV canonization, were a more cruel and vindictive race than the Delawares. Outrages were committed on their victims that could not be printed in the newspapers of the time or even today. Most Indian tribes had the misguided custom of inflicting

---

3. "As It Was in the Beginning" is told from the point of view of Foard Hudspeth, a white trader who tries to outdo Shaved Head, a Comanche Indian, in a trade involving a white girl whom the Comanches have raised after killing her parents.

punishment on an innocent white man they could catch for the wrongs inflicted on them by white men who escaped them. But the Delaware had a form of quasi-legal reasoning, often with an explanation and an expressed regret for the necessity of what they had to do. On the other hand, the Apaches and frequently the Comanches fell on their victims like wolves.

Q. In addition to trying to be fair to both sides in *The Light in the Forest*—to presenting the contrasting values of two societies—I wonder if you also thought of the novel as a story of "growing up." The epigraph from Wordsworth might suggest this.[4]

A. The Wordsworth quotation should suggest to the reader a great deal that should not be made banal by explanation. In my own case the transition from the freedom, ease, and youthful companionship in high school to confinement in the Vulcan depths of a dark, smelly, smoky and seemingly purposeless machine shop, all of this at the age of fifteen, was a rude awakening and difficult adjustment. In answer to letters, I have occasionally counseled young inquirers to appreciate and make the most of their youth, warning them that they will look back on it some day as trailing clouds of glory, as Wordsworth did. I doubt if my letters convinced a single youth. The gods-that-be evidently discovered the intransigence of man aeons ago and came to the conclusion that rude experience and harsh deprivement were the only things that worked upon him.

Q. Did you write *The Light in the Forest,* then, with the idea of appealing to adolescent readers?

A. No. The novel was written for adults. I had no thought of appealing to adolescents.

Q. When you were writing the novel, were you at all tempted to end it with True Son's return to the Indians at the end of Chapter Thirteen? Why did you feel the novel could not end there?

A. Such a happy ending would not have satisfied the purpose of an artist or have been true to life.

Q. At the end of *The Light in the Forest,* True Son, rejecting one society and rejected by the other, appears to be left only with Nature. Do you consider the ending tragic?

A. This question and others like it have been asked me by

---

4. Shades of the prison-house begin to close
   Upon the growing Boy,
But he beholds the light, and whence it flows,
   He sees it in his joy.

                  —Wordsworth
                "Ode: Intimations of Immortality"

many students and some of their teachers. The ending is indeed tragic but not planned for that purpose. Not until the book was published and sales grew and letters arrived did I realize its value in mildly shocking the reader and making him question and think.

Q. Edwin Gaston says that you attribute your "polished style . . . largely to journalism."[5] It seems to me, however, that much of the effectiveness of *The Light in the Forest* comes from the irony in the contrasts between white and Indian ways of life— presumably not a journalistic quality. Can you state more precisely what your work as a journalist taught you about writing?

A. Gaston came to see me once. It was more of a social call with his wife and sons. He asked few questions. My agent was shown a copy of the manuscript by the publisher and he sent it on to me. I did not read it but my wife and daughter did and asked if they might correct many mistakes which the publisher, probably after consultation with Gaston, declined to allow. Gaston did ask me to confirm a few details of his own. What you mention is one of the uncorrected errors. My newspaper work gave me a certain facility in writing, also excellent training in turning out work with or without inspiration and whether I felt like it or not, but there is little resemblance between my newspaper and novel styles.

Q. In writing your novels do you think of the chapter as the most important structural unit or do you conceive of the novel in larger segments?

A. My novels may be said to follow two designs. One, as in *The Trees, The Fields, The Town,* and *A Simple Honorable Man,* advances the purpose and progress of the novel in individual chapters, each telling a story of its own but contributing gradually to the whole. The other method is the straight narrative or story, as in *The Sea of Grass, The Lady,* and *The Light in the Forest.*

Q. Some of these novels have been made into motion pictures, but I understand that you have not been interested in seeing them. Do you feel that the motion picture as an art form is generally incapable of successfully adapting novels?

A. I worked on several assignments in the MGM Studio in the thirties and saw how reputable novels were turned into films that bore little resemblance to the story or credibility of the original work. This was done to please other minds that might include not only half a dozen different studio adapters but the producer, director, and assistant producer and director along with their wives, all of whom wanted to have a hand in it. I understand the moving picture version of *The Light in the Forest* is no exception to this.

5. Gaston, *Conrad Richter,* p. 28.

Q. Both critics and teachers have found the novel a rather slippery form to define—when does a long short story become a novelette? Is length the only distinguishing factor? Does your original conception of a work include an idea of its length and scope?

A. You ask about the novel and novelette. If the novel is in the plan of *War and Peace,* the difference is obvious. In the case of narrative, as *The Light in the Forest,* length is a distinguishing factor. My novel *The Sea of Grass* was written as a short story but grew too long, and yet has turned out to be one of my most successful novels—reprinted to date in the original edition some thirteen or fourteen times, [and] published in many foreign translations and in other editions in English by six or eight different publishers.

Q. In view of the difficulties in defining the novel and in dealing in classes with longer works of literature, what do you think of as the most important things for a teacher to do? How can he help his students to "see" a novel in its entirety?

A. All novels, I think, can be reduced to a simple theme and purpose academically. I would rather see students taught and infected with an intimate interest in and understanding of the characters and story, together with some appreciation of the art of good writing. Years ago in my home town two sisters now gone taught in high school and I still hear their praises sung by former students. A rough Pennsylvania Dutchman once called my attention with pride to the sunset and informed me that Miss Boyer had taught him as a boy to see its beauty, that he had never noticed such things before.

ALAN PATON

Photo: Katharine Young

Alan Paton was born January 11, 1903, in Pietermaritzburg, South Africa. He attended Maritzburg College from 1914–1918, and the University of Natal from which he obtained a B.Sc. in 1923.

From 1925 to 1935 he taught in high school and in college, becoming increasingly interested in the underprivileged. This interest led to a position as principal of Diepkloof Reformatory, a prison school for delinquent black boys near Johannesburg, where Paton remained, instituting reforms, until 1948.

During the fifties Paton was instrumental in founding the Liberal party of South Africa, whose national president he later became. This party, which advocated political rights for all South Africans, to be accompanied by the economic integration of all South Africa's people, was finally declared illegal in 1968.

Paton's first novel, *Cry, the Beloved Country,* was written during a 1947 trip to Europe and America to study penal practices and was published in 1948 by Charles Scribner's Sons. It was soon recognized as a classic and has found its way into both high school and college curriculums. A second novel, *Too Late the Phalarope,* appeared in 1953 from Scribner. Paton's other writing includes short stories (*Tales from a Troubled Land,* Scribner, 1961), a biography of South African statesman Jan Hofmeyr (Oxford University Press, 1964), and other works of nonfiction dealing with South Africa and particularly her political and social problems (*The Land and the People of South Africa,* J. B. Lippincott Company, 1955; *South Africa in Transition,* Scribner, 1956; *Hope for South Africa,* Frederick Praeger, Inc., 1959). In collaboration with Krishna Shah he wrote a play based on three of his short stories (*Sponono,* Scribner, 1965).

Paton is the winner of numerous awards and honors, including the Anisfield-Wolf *Saturday Review* Award in 1948, the Newspaper Guild of New York Page One Award in 1949, and the London Sunday *Times* Special Award for Literature in 1949—all for *Cry, the Beloved Country.* He was also granted the Freedom House Award in 1960, the Medal for Literature, Free Academy of Arts in 1961, and the C.N.A. Literary Award for the year's best book in English in South Africa, for *Hofmeyr* in 1965.

Paton married Doris Francis in 1928; she died in 1967. They had two sons. In 1969 Paton married Anne Hopkins. They make their home in Botha's Hill, Natal, South Africa.

An Interview with Alan Paton

Q. Each school year many high school teachers in America teach *Cry, the Beloved Country* in their classes. Do you have any special advice, any special cautions for them?

A. I don't know that I would have any special advice or cautions for American teachers of *Cry, the Beloved Country,* except to say that it was written twenty-two years ago and many things have altered since then and many have not. I will content myself by mentioning only one thing and that is that the day of African political movements is for the moment over. The penalties, most of them extralegal, which can be imposed on opponents of the Government are so drastic that all African political activity has either been driven underground or has ceased to exist.

Q. Does this mean, then, that *Cry, the Beloved Country* would differ if you were writing it today?

A. Yes, *Cry, the Beloved Country* would differ greatly if I were to write it today. This, however, would be due far less to the changing circumstances of the country than to the changes in myself. I would not be capable of the same intensity of emotion as I was then.

Q. But even today the book has both immediate social and political overtones as well as universal qualities. Should the teacher emphasize the immediate or should he emphasize the universal?

A. I should say he should not emphasize one more than the other, but I am not necessarily the best judge. When I look back upon this book which I have not read for more than twenty years I would say that these two things are inseparable. It was a book written about a certain country and its aim was to tell a true story about that country. My own firm belief is that a writer must, above all, tell a story and that the rules of story telling are the most important rules for him, far more important than presenting some point of view or policy. If he does present some point of view or policy, then that is because he is the kind of person that he is. We have one or two authors who write stories about South Africa and steer clear of anything which might be called controversial. Such books are generally quite insipid. On the other hand any story written about South Africa whose aim is to lambaste the Government and one's opponents is equally irritating to any discerning reader.

Q. How does the novelist go about finding a story to tell? Do

This "interview" was conducted through correspondence during 1967–1968. Mr. Paton replied to a number of written questions and then approved an edited version of his responses.

you think you would have become a novelist if you had not lived in South Africa?

A. I am quite sure that a professional novelist must very often go consciously searching for a subject. You ask if I would have become a novelist if I had not lived in South Africa. This reminds me of the question put to a friend of mine: he was asked "If you did not live in South Africa where would you like to live?" and his reply was "If I did not live in South Africa I would like to live in South Africa." He received a deserved ovation for this reply. I think it very probable that I would have wanted to write in any country and writing is still my favorite form of self-expression.

Q. You've made comments on the South African background for *Cry, the Beloved Country* in the introduction to the Scribner Modern Standard Authors edition. You talk about the changes in the way of life of the black people, the movement toward the cities, the weakening of tribal controls, the increase of crime and misery. "This," you say, "is the central theme of my novel."

A. Yes.

Q. I wonder, however, if you haven't given a more inclusive statement about the novel's theme in another context. In an article in *The Christian Century* (March 8, 1950), entitled "Toward a Spiritual Community," you said:

> It is a well-known fact that when a powerful magnet is brought near to a haphazard assemblage of iron filings, they will, if they are free to move, arrange themselves immediately in the field of its attraction. They take upon themselves a pattern whose unity and direction are clearly discernible. Some may be unable to respond. There may be qualities of roughness and unevenness in the surface on which they lie, and these local and immediate obstructions may prevent individuals form responding to the greater and more powerful attractions. Others, ready to respond, may be prevented by those that obstruct them, weigh down upon them and otherwise hinder them. Still others may contain impurities that prevent them from fully responding.

You go on to say, "This is a picture of the human world," but isn't it a peculiarly apt description of the special world of *Cry, the Beloved Country*—and also of *Too Late the Phalarope*?

A. I think the answer is that the comment in the introduction to the Scribner edition is on a very different plane from the comment in the article in *The Christian Century*. I am sure that the second comment would have been quite unsuitable for the Scribner introduction. I would not have thought of the second comment as a peculiarly apt description of the special world of both my novels. I would stand by my statement that the second comment is in fact "a picture of the human world." If it should happen that this appears a peculiarly apt description of my own special world, I would take this as a great compliment and consider that I had related the particular to the universal with some success.

Q. There are certainly elements in *Cry, the Beloved Country* which are universal or archetypal in prose fiction—the journey, the relationship of father and son, to name but two. How far does the South African context modify these universals? To what degree do you feel they become local and unique themes?

A. You are quite right about the archetypal elements in *Cry, the Beloved Country*. The South African context modifies these universals in exactly the same way that any other context would modify them. Someone wrote to me on this same topic the other day in connection with *Too Late the Phalarope*, and I replied that I myself would find it almost impossible to write a novel that did not concern itself with the father/son, mother/son, brother/brother, brother/sister, aunt/nephew, and similar family relationships. I remember being very strongly drawn to John Updike's story, *The Centaur*, which deals with the tender relationship of an ineffectual school master to his son who suffers from a skin condition of which he is very much ashamed. Sometimes when I read stories which do not say anything about these relationships at all (I exclude short stories), I find myself wondering why family life has so little affected the writer. I can only suppose that my own family life as a child, and later as a husband and father, must have meant more to me than it meant to such a writer. This is so tremendous a question that one cannot really do justice to it in a few words.

Q. I'd like to explore a little further how you go about writing a novel. Novelists as far back as Fielding have thought and spoken of themselves as "biographers" and "historians". You have written a real biography—*Hofmeyr*—and a good deal of real history—*Hope for South Africa*, etc. When you write a novel, do you think of yourself as a "biographer" or "historian" in any sense?

A. When I write a novel I do not think of myself as a biographer or an historian, but I will admit that when I write a biography, the novelist is very much to the fore. He has to hold himself in check because he must not invent anything, but he wants to make his biography essentially the story of a man. I think this was true of Sandburg's *Lincoln:* I think in fact it is true of any

great biography. When I read R. Blake's life of Disraeli I felt that
the biographer had failed altogether to give the picture of a man.
When I wrote *Hofmeyr,* although I certainly tried to give an account of the times in which he lived, and although I regarded this
as an essential part of the biography, it was something quite different that made the book exciting to me. His rebellion against, and
submissiveness to, his mother; his passionate love of cricket which
he could not play very well; his love of boys and boys' games and
boys' clubs which, if it was homosexual, was never so in any active
sense; his extraordinary powers of memory; his great blunder at
the University; his puritanical morality mixed up with really important morality; his tremendous appetite and his ugly way of eating; his meanness over money and then his giving up four fifths of
his salary to a special trust fund for African education when he felt
that he had saved enough; all these things absolutely fascinated me
and this was largely because I am a story teller.

Q.   The good biographer must be a good story teller then?

A.   Yes. I am inclined to believe that it is distinction between
fact and fiction that separates the biography from the novel, and I
still adhere to my contention that the more a biography takes of the
nature of a story, the better it is.

Q.   You say the biographer, however, "must not invent anything." Are there limits to what the novelist can properly invent?
Does the novelist have an obligation to be objective?

A.   I don't think so. I have a great admiration for Thomas
Wolfe who was anything but objective. On the whole, however, the
great novelists have been objective writers. I think it was George
Meredith who said that the mark of the great writer was a mascu-
line objectivity.

Q.   Are there different kinds of objectivity for a novelist?

A.   I am sure that there are. The wholly objective writer like
Proust is much admired by me, but I would not wish to write like
that. It seems to me that an extreme objectivity of this kind must
necessarily be accompanied by a kind of clinical coldness.

Q.   How far is the novelist free to use devices—like coincidence—which would undermine objectivity?

A.   The use of coincidence in a novel is, I am sure, quite
legitimate, but highly dangerous. I cannot remember the name of
the novelist who protested to a critic, "But this really happened;" to
which the critic replied, "Whether it happened or not it has no
place in the novel."

Q.   What you say seems to suggest that you don't try to be
objective in your novels. Yet, ostensibly, the point of view in *Cry,*

the Beloved Country is that of third person narrative told by an omniscient author. Do you conceive of your narrator as a character in any sense?

A. I am often asked whether the narrator of *Cry, the Beloved Country* is not really the young man who was murdered. I suppose that to some extent this is inevitable. I don't know whether any writer can keep himself wholly out of his books, but would think it highly improbable.

Q. It seems to me that the good teacher will take this into account and make his students aware of point of view. What else should he be sure they notice? For example, the apparent structure of *Cry, the Beloved Country* lies in its division into three books with their differing points of focus on the two families. Is this kind of analysis the most useful, or should the teacher concentrate on other things—for example, the structure underneath the surface structure which is suggested by the patterning of scenes of emotional climax?

A. I don't think that the division of *Cry, the Beloved Country* into three books is without its significance, but I certainly do not think that the teacher should dwell upon it.

Q. Most teachers *will* dwell on the style of the book, I think. Critics have called it "poetic" and you yourself have written poetry. Do you think this is an accurate description of your novels? Do you consciously strive for "poetic" qualities?

A. If I am to judge from the opinions of a great number of people, then my writing can be called poetic. I don't, however, consciously strive to achieve these qualities, and I think that if I did it would very soon become evident. As you no doubt know, I write best under the influence of emotion; this leads some people to call my writing sentimental, but in my own humble opinion these people don't so much dislike the style as they dislike the theme.

Q. Does the style come partly from a kind of translation or transformation of African languages or is it your invention apart from such influences?

A. I would not think that it was due to the influence of any African language except in respect to the dialogue. I cannot say that it was my invention, because any invention is a conscious process, whereas the style of *Cry, the Beloved Country* comes from the unconscious.

Q. Are there any literary influences that may have stimulated this unconscious process?

A. I suppose inevitably it was influenced by the Bible. There were two things that created in me the urge to write the novel: one was being homesick in Norway just after having seen what must be one of the most beautiful rose windows in the world in the Cathedral at Trondheim, the other was having encountered for the first time Steinbeck's *Grapes of Wrath.* I would not say, however, that Steinbeck's manner of writing influenced me at all, and I think that the style was my own.

Q. You mention Steinbeck as one of the American novelists who has impressed you. Are there other American novelists who seem to be trying to give the same kind of interpretation of America and its problems that you have given for South Africa, especially in racial terms?

A. There are obviously some American novelists who are extremely concerned about the problems of their country and culture, and I don't need to tell you that these are not necessarily the best novelists. Besides Steinbeck's *Grapes of Wrath,* I think, for example, of Lillian Smith, of Baldwin and Langston Hughes and Wright. Faulkner of course wrote a great deal of the country and its problems into his novels, but I don't think he was as emotionally involved as those others were. I also got a strong impression when I visited America ten years ago that the problems of race were not felt anything like as keenly as they are felt today, and I think this new concern may manifest itself more and more.

Q. Are there other things about American writers that have impressed you?

A. There was another thing that struck me very much about the American novel, and that was that it could draw on a much greater complexity of material than South African writers could do. So rich was the material that many of them could omit the racial problems of their country altogether and yet not seem to be avoiding them. That is not true here. Those writers who tell South African stories without any apparent recognition of these problems are thought by persons like myself to be extremely shallow. What is more, South African writers today are afraid in the first place of offending white sensitivities and in the second place are afraid because a book may be banned on the slightest pretext, and in fact is much more likely to be banned if it deals with race than if it deals with sex, which is very odd for a Calvinist country. I think the American novelist is fortunate to live in a country which allows almost complete freedom in the criticism of itself and its government and its policies.

Q. I think we in America have been struck, however, both at the boldness with which you have spoken out about the situation in South Africa and by the way that your analysis of that situation has shaped your development as a writer. For example, in an article in the *Saturday Review* of May 2, 1953, entitled "South Africa—the White Man's Dilemma," you gave an analysis of present tendencies and at the same time suggested a provocative theory of tragedy:

> It will be seen therefore that the white man in South Africa is really in a dilemma, but it might be questioned whether it is tragic. It might still be argued that it is a dilemma of racial arrogance and selfishness. But suppose it could be shown that the resistances preventing a solution are not easily amenable to reason, but are altogether deeper? This I fear they are.

Later in the essay you say, "Human life is a strange mixture, never fully explained or understood, of freedoms and bondages." Can you elaborate on this? For example, are arrogance and selfishness in the area of choice, of freedom?

A. I would say that they are, but where the fundamental cause is fear, where one is arrogant and selfish because one fears for oneself and for one's own security, then they are much more difficult to deal with. I think it would be agreed that very few fears can be reasoned with. St. John wrote that only perfect love can cast out fear and to me this is the plain and simple truth, but it does not necessarily make the solution any easier. The bondages that go deeper than reason are to my mind always related to fear.

Q. As a novelist you must have had to find some balance between freedom and bondage in creating your characters. How did you go about this?

A. I cannot answer that, but I would like to quote something which I wrote recently:

> When I was a young man, my student days over, I was influenced for a while by an unwilling belief in a rigid determinism, that choice and will were illusory, that we are what we are because of all the external forces that made us: our parents, friends, school, society, world, our physiology and our metabolism, and all the rest of them. I lived in a race-caste society, and I was determined to get out of it, although it was physically more comfortable to live in it, to identify with it, even to be ready to die for it. What force was working there inside me? Was it simply another product of parents, friends, school, society, world, physiology, metabolism? Yes, in a way it was. But today I believe that was nothing more than an out-view, one which saw myself as a tool, a toy, a thing to be moved about by forces external to myself. Today I do not underestimate

these external forces; today I hold an in-view, one which sees myself as a self, made no doubt by many forces beyond my control, but gaining in coherence and integrity as I grow older. I am no longer a determinist: I am, in so far as a man can be, a self-determinator. That is one of the freedoms that the gospel gives to us, a belief in our worth as persons, a belief in what we can *do* as persons, a belief in what we can *be*. And no one helped me more to understand it than Francis of Assisi.[1]

Q.   The relationship between freedom and bondage, between self-determination and determinism is one that teachers often discuss in connection with tragedy, whether in drama or in fiction. Your work would seem to suggest that you feel more at home in the tragic mode.

A.   It is true that in writing I feel more at home in the tragic mode, but this is not true in conversation at all. I am very fond of witty and humorous conversation.

Q.   Do you think tragedy is a more significant mode? Does it offer more possibilities for a writer who has something to say?

A.   I don't think it is necessarily more significant. I think that to be able to write real comedy can be a gift just as great as writing tragedy. In fact I don't think one understands life properly unless one sees it as both comic and tragic. I would even doubt if tragedy offers more possibilities to a writer who has something to say. I would venture a last generalization, namely that the world has produced far more great writers of tragedy than great writers of comedy.

Q.   Do you think that tragedy works out differently in the novel and the drama? For example, were you happy with Maxwell Anderson's stage adaptation of your novel?

A.   When I first saw a rehearsal I was quite numbed, but this was partly due to the fact that he created for his play an atmosphere that corresponded to no reality that I knew. Once I got used to this I was able to see it as a work of art existing in its own right. I learnt one lesson from this, and that is that when an author sells his book he should have as little to do with the dramatization or the filming as possible. Some authors won't go near the cinema or theatre at all, and I can quite understand this feeling. Anderson did, however, impose upon the play something which was his own, not mine at all, and this is made evident by the title which he gave his play, *Lost in the Stars.* He was the son of a Baptist minister and

1. Alan Paton, *Instrument of Thy Peace* (New York: The Seabury Press, Inc., 1967).

turned against religion in a very strange way. It was not that he ceased to believe in God but rather that he felt that God had made the world and then gone away. I think this emerges very clearly towards the end of the play.

Q. Apparently this experience didn't make you feel that your work was unsuited to dramatic adaptation, since you collaborated on the dramatic version of a group of your short stories—*Sponono.*

A. Actually, I don't think that I am a good collaborator in adapting any writing of mine for stage or screen. *Sponono* was made with two motives: the first one was creative; the second was to make a play which would give an opportunity for African actors, and in this it was supremely successful. One of the reasons why I enjoyed this particular piece of collaboration was because I worked with a young Indian director, Krishna Shah, for whom I felt a great affinity. If the opportunity presented itself—which does not seem likely—of working with him again, I would probably take it, but otherwise I would never attempt any more work of this kind.

Q. From your collaboration in the dramatic version of *Sponono,* would you say there are advantages in the points of view that a writer may take in the novel over those possible in drama? Does drama offer less freedom?

A. Undoubtedly there are advantages in the novel. The drama offers far less freedom than the novel, but on the other hand, it is its extraordinary compactness that gives it such power and strength. Very few plays succeed unless they conform to these rigid demands. Almost every line in a play must be a preparation for something still to come. This is not necessarily true of the novel, although there are novels, such as those of Conrad for example, which must be read with the utmost concentration; otherwise the whole story will elude the reader. I think *Heart of Darkness* is a striking example of this. I tried to read it easily and casually and I missed the whole story. It was my son who persuaded me to try again and it was only then that I understood the story.

Q. You raise an interesting issue for teachers. Some teachers believe a novel should not be presented to a student until he is ready to grasp its full implications and feel its total impact. Others argue that some novels at least can be successfully taught at different levels in different ways. They would cite the fact that *Huckleberry Finn* is taught all the way from junior high school to graduate school. Which position comes closer to your view?

A. I agree with those teachers who believe that some novels can be successfully taught at different levels in different ways, and strangely enough, I would also have used *Huckleberry Finn* as an example. This is also certainly true of *Alice in Wonderland* which, as you may know, was recently presented by the British Broadcasting Corporation featuring such persons as John Gielgud and Malcolm Muggeridge. The presentation created quite a sensation, as it gave quite a new level of meaning to this extraordinary book.

Q. Do you think that *Cry, the Beloved Country* could be successfully presented at different levels?

A. Yes. If any proof is required of this, I still to this very day receive letters about the book from writers whose ages vary from fourteen to eighty.

Q. You yourself once taught English. What do you feel are the most important experiences for students to get from a work of literature—specifically a novel—perhaps at any level?

A. When I taught English I tried to get my pupils to grow excited over the use of words and the use of language; to distinguish between the clear and vivid and moving way of saying something and the dull and unimaginative way of saying it, and to be excited about good poetry. I have a friend who has taught English all his life and can infect even the most unlikely boys with his enthusiasm. It seems to me that this infection with enthusiasm is the most important experience that a student can have, but it does not relate specifically to the novel, it relates specifically to language and words.

JOHN KNOWLES

John Knowles was born September 16, 1926, in Fairmont, West Virginia. After a boyhood in that state, he entered Phillips Exeter Academy, which he transferred "brick for brick," as he says, when he created the school which is the setting for *A Separate Peace.* Graduating from Exeter in 1945, he went on to Yale University, where he obtained his B.A. in 1949.

After graduating from college he worked briefly as a newspaper reporter in Hartford, Connecticut, then as a free-lance writer and, from 1956 to 1960, as an associate editor for *Holiday Magazine.*

A Separate Peace, published by The Macmillan Company, appeared in 1960 and remains the best known of his novels. It won the Rosenthal Award of the National Institute of Arts and Letters and the William Faulkner Foundation Award, both in 1960, and has been acclaimed by the *Times Literary Supplement* as "a novel of altogether exceptional power and distinction." It has found its way into the curriculums of both high schools and colleges as rapidly as any book in our time.

Knowles' second novel, *Morning in Antibes* (Macmillan, 1962), as well as a work of nonfiction, *Double Vision: American Thoughts Abroad* (Macmillan, 1964), came out of his extensive travels in Europe and the Mediterranean. A third novel, *Indian Summer,* was published by Random House in 1966. His latest novel, *The Paragon,* appeared in 1971 from Random House.

Knowles is also the author of short stories which have appeared in *New World Writing, Story,* and other magazines. "Phineas," a short story on which *A Separate Peace* was based, has been published in a collection with five other stories written between 1951 and 1967 (Random House, 1968).

Mr. Knowles makes his home on Long Island, New York.

An Interview with John Knowles

HOWES. Mr. Knowles, your novel, *A Separate Peace*, has been widely taught in many different kinds of secondary school classes, ranging all the way from ninth grade to twelfth grade, from classes of general students to advanced placement classes. Do you have any feelings about where and how it might be taught most appropriately?

KNOWLES. I just wish it wouldn't be taught to students very young. I don't see how they can understand it. After all, the novel is told from the perspective of an adult.

HOWES. How young is too young? Are high school students incapable of understanding this adult perspective?

KNOWLES. No, high school isn't too young. I've received many letters from ninth-grade students who seem to have had a tremendous response to the book. I suspect they're not seeing everything, however, and I hope they will go back, perhaps at twenty-one or twenty-five, and read the book again with a perspective on their own adolescence. What is interesting is that the ninth- and tenth-grade girls tend to fall in love with Phineas and the boys tend to identify with Phineas or Gene or both. And I have had hundreds of letters from high school students saying they have had a friend like Phineas, so that in that age group there is a powerful emotional involvement in the novel, and it works well. Therefore, I'm not opposed to its being taught to them, but I think they will have a rather different experience if they read it again when they're older.

HOWES. Do you feel that it is beyond the grasp of non-college-bound students, students who wouldn't have any knowledge of the prep school world of Devon?

KNOWLES. Envy is not restricted to the college-bound, nor is the violence in the human heart unknown to people who have never heard of a prep school.

HOWES. If then—God forbid, I suppose you would say—if you had to teach your novel to some particular class, how would you start?

KNOWLES. Just by reading it. Of course I would not teach what I have written, so that is a hypothetical question. I really wouldn't have the slightest idea of how to teach what I have written because I wouldn't see any other perspective than my own perspective in writing it, and that experience is the book itself. I wouldn't have any notion how to teach it. . . . But I was a lecturer in creative

This interview took place in New York City on December 16, 1968.

writing at Princeton last year and I had two seminars. We did discuss one of my short stories, "The Reading of the Will," and we dealt with it structurally. Why did I develop this kind of character? (He has just lost his father.) Why was he put in that setting? (We see him in the death-dominated culture of Egypt.) And how does the interaction of character and culture produce plot and theme? So I would approach *A Separate Peace* the same way. How is it constructed and why?

HOWES. This meeting of the "culture" or the setting and the character must have been a major concern in *A Separate Peace.*

KNOWLES. Yes. I brought together an aggressive streak—in Gene—in the most meaningful setting of an overwhelmingly peaceful prep school, and a singularly nonaggressive spirit—Phineas— and surrounded them with the raging of World War II. The war comes in more and more, it gathers and gathers until it takes over the campus in the parachute riggers' school.

HOWES. Do readers of the novel tend to overlook the importance of the war?

KNOWLES. You don't have to become conscious of it in reading the novel, but if it is subjected to formal study, this element would be brought to life.

HOWES. Would part of the teacher's job be, then, to point out the surrounding context of the war?

KNOWLES. Yes. It's the concept of a personality, Gene, juxtaposed with a world having the same weaknesses as that personality.

HOWES. Are there other important things in the novel that tend to be overlooked?

KNOWLES. Yes. One other obvious strain which seems to be overlooked is the classical Greek allusions. I tried to keep everything as simple as I could, but I couldn't avoid seeing the connection between the novel I found myself writing and classical Greece. I was well along in the book before I discerned the connection, but there is the burning of the *Iliad,* the Grecian sunlight in Vermont. I tried to keep this unobtrusive, but whenever possible to indicate the parallels. The most prevalent view of the critics is that there are symbols drawn from Christianity, but no one has brought up the classical Greek links.

HOWES. In a piece called "The Young Writer's Real Friends,"[1] you said that "if anything as I wrote *A Separate Peace* tempted me to insert artificial complexities, I ignored it. If anything appeared which looked suspiciously like a symbol, I left it on its own." Yet

1. Reprinted in *The Writer* (July 1962), pp. 12–14, 37, from the *New York Times Book Review.*

critics have used phrases about your work like "dramatizes the myths of America's youth" and "new allegory of American life." You say that you tried to keep symbol and allusion unobtrusive in *A Separate Peace*. What is the place of symbols in a novel?

KNOWLES. Symbols and myths only work if they are part of the writer's mind. If they are forced—schematically, artificially—on the material, it will be dead. You don't have to put symbols into novels, because the human mind only works symbolically and it is impossible to write a novel that doesn't acquire a symbolic strain.

HOWES. Many teachers start their discussions of novels not with symbols, but with questions on the details in the story, the point of view, the qualities and motives of the characters. Do questions of this sort seem to you to be good ways of approaching a novel?

KNOWLES. Yes. Questions like that seem to be a way of breaking down the book and getting students to think about it.

HOWES. But is there a danger of too much "breaking down," too much analysis?

KNOWLES. That goes without saying.

HOWES. Is there any other way of approaching a novel which would avoid the danger of overanalysis?

KNOWLES. I know how to write books, I don't know how to teach them. . . . But I think a novel should be taken at face value first—as an experience. And then you might go on to the reverberations. You start with a very special concrete set of people and experiences. That is, in the first instance, what counts. And it is the primary value of my books anyway. Then, if you want to go on into the underlying reverberations and themes as secondary values, fine. But it's important to keep that order straight. A student told me once, when writing an examination on *Tender Is the Night*, "Well, of course Nicole Diver is crass materialism." There was something wrong in his mind or in the way he was taught that book. Fitzgerald himself was utterly opposed to that way of reading and writing. He said that if you begin with a symbol, you end with nothing, but if you begin with people, you may end with symbols, provided you're not aiming toward them.

HOWES. I assume from your statement that you have an admiration for Fitzgerald.

KNOWLES. Yes, very much.

HOWES. And likewise that you admire Hemingway, since the title for *A Separate Peace* is found in his *In Our Time*.

KNOWLES. The title does not come from Hemingway. The title and everything in *A Separate Peace* come from life and not from other books. When *A Separate Peace* was taking shape in my mind,

I remembered that Italy had signed a separate peace in World War II and I found the title there. Years later I ran across the phrase in Hemingway. Devon, brick for brick and leaf for leaf, is Exeter. It comes from life. *A Separate Peace* is, of course, related in an indirect way to other books, but it is based on Exeter and my experience during World War II.

HOWES. What about the people in the book? Were they based on real people?

KNOWLES. Was there a Phineas? People often ask me this and their curiosity is natural. Like all writers who write a novel which works, I put something of myself into all the major characters. One definition of a novelist, you know, is a person with more than normal facets to himself. Maybe Tolstoy is the greatest novelist and maybe that's the reason he became everyone in *War and Peace* from Natasha to Napoleon. That is the underlying way the novelist constructs character. Then, of course, you do often choose someone to model. You become the glue to hold the character together, but it can be based on someone. Phineas has been publicly identified as based on David Hackett, who was a member of a United States Olympic hockey team and a close associate of Robert Kennedy. But the question ought to be irrelevant, don't you think?

HOWES. Yes. After all, whatever the source, he exists in the context of the novel.

KNOWLES. Yes. It's a question whether the novel should be broken into its raw materials that way. I understand the curiosity and am pleased by it, but I don't want to take part in the breaking down. . . .

HOWES. Would you be willing to talk about *A Separate Peace* by breaking it down from another point of view? How did your short story, "Phineas," grow into the novel, *A Separate Peace?*

KNOWLES. The story began actually with "A Turn with the Sun," which showed me I had a great deal of feeling about Exeter. In trying to understand those feelings, I wrote "Phineas." Still not having understood, I expanded "Phineas" to *A Separate Peace* . . . and then I understood.

HOWES. What were those feelings?

KNOWLES. Feelings about the school, about that period in my life, about that period in history—that is, World War II—and feelings about that period in everybody's life—adolescence.

HOWES. Aubrey Menen speaks for many critics in thinking of *A Separate Peace* as a tragedy. He says: "Beginning with a tiny incident among ordinary boys, it ends by being as deep and as big as evil itself. As I read the story I had the feeling of climbing a tower and looking at wider and wider prospects of human nature, each bleaker than the last. . . . The characters are real, the tragedy is inevitable. . . ." Was part of what happened between "Phineas" and *A Separate Peace* that the story turned into a tragedy as your feelings changed?

KNOWLES. My feelings didn't change, but I got a deeper insight into the two people and their relationship. I hadn't fully explored my emotions when I wrote the short story. In expanding the story to the novel, it took on the dimensions of tragedy.

HOWES. When did you decide Phineas had to die?

KNOWLES. As I was writing the novel it became clear that to be true to life as I understand it, he would have to die. Life tends to destroy people like that—if not physically, then spiritually. But it isn't just Phineas's story, though readers sometimes misunderstand Gene. You know that sentence on the last page—"Because my war ended before I ever put on a uniform; I was on active duty all my time at school; I killed my enemy there." Let me ask you what you think it means.

HOWES. I think the enemy is Gene's self-ignorance.

KNOWLES. Exactly. And fourteen-year-olds don't make the mistake of thinking the enemy is Phineas. It takes scholarship to do that.

HOWES. Does that account also for the point of view—the fact that the story is told by an older Gene?

KNOWLES. Yes. It's important to show that Gene had not been destroyed by the tragedy, but had incorporated it into himself and his own understanding of life.

HOWES. The dust jacket of your collection of short stories just published, *Phineas,* points out that "*A Separate Peace* has become, along with *The Catcher in the Rye* and *Lord of the Flies,* one of the most influential books in schools and colleges throughout the country." Do you see the three books as sharing a common purpose in any way in speaking for or to the younger generation?

KNOWLES. Of course *Catcher in the Rye* was written years before *A Separate Peace.* I was already planning *A Separate Peace* when *Catcher* came out, and I deliberately didn't read *Catcher* until I had finished *A Separate Peace,* so as not to be influenced. I am an admirer of *Catcher,* but it has almost no resemblance to my book except for the prep school setting. *Lord of the Flies* is so heavily allegorical that it is not my cup of tea as a novel. The only connection among the three, if there is one, is the view of latent hostility, aggressiveness, destructiveness in adolescence . . . in humanity, in reality. All three are very well written, if I do say so. And I think adolescents respond to well-written books.

HOWES. Did you write *A Separate Peace* with an adolescent audience partly in mind?

KNOWLES. No, I didn't think it would appeal to adolescents. I was not sure it would even be published, and I thought it would have at best a small readership. I have been surprised. After one year it was still alive. Now, nine years later, it is more alive than ever. I thought it was a wonderful book, but I didn't think anyone else would think so. I think my other books are of the same general level, and I have been curious as to why *A Separate Peace* is so popular. I suppose it's partly the importance of the author's voice. The first hearing of an author's own distinct voice makes an impact and after that anything is anticlimactic.

HOWES. Your mention of the author's voice suggests an attitude about the novel as a form. What differences do you see between the novel and other genres?

KNOWLES. The novel is the most intimate of the extended forms of prose. That's why I like it best. The short story and the novella are fragmentary; the play is public; the poem can't be sustained. You get closer to the reader for longer in the novel than in any other form.

HOWES. But this very advantage presents problems for the teacher. How can he deal with the problem of length in a class? How can he help students to see a novel in its entirety?

KNOWLES. Choose short novels, for one thing. When I went to school, we read *A Lost Lady* and other short novels. But there's no easy way around the problem, no royal road to learning. You have to plug away and most don't do it.

HOWES. And the plugging away, it seems to me, may bar adolescents from entering the world of a novel. If there's too much analysis, their interest may flag.

KNOWLES. Well, read it for what it is, for the characters and situations, for what it tells about their lives and lives in general. Then you can hold their attention. If you want to go to "higher criticism" afterwards, then it's all right.

HOWES. But you would stop short of that with tenth graders, for example.

KNOWLES. Yes.

HOWES. How much partial understanding, then, would you settle for?

KNOWLES. Can the last page of *A Separate Peace* be understood by adolescents—that is, can they understand that people construct resistances to aggressiveness only to find that the aggressiveness is in themselves, and that the effort of self-defense is more destructive than any outward attack? I don't believe that most can, but this merely means that they should read the book again at twenty-five.

HOWES. I suppose the novel offers different readers different things anyway, doesn't it? It's always seemed to me that the novel as a genre is a curious hybrid in some ways, with elements of history, biography, the essay. Do you see these elements in the novel?

KNOWLES. Yes. The subtitle of *Madame Bovary* is "Moeurs de Province." It's one of the endearing things about the novel: many novelists have thought of themselves as historians, biographers, portrayers of manners. The novel was read in the nineteenth century for such things as the picture of Dickens' London, for its informational side. This journalistic or sociological value helps to explain the novel's popularity. Today, that role has been superseded by newspapers, magazines, TV, and this fact has brought on the so-called crisis in the novel. Is it losing its role? It's not losing it, but is changing and becoming a prolonged intimacy between author and reader. It's becoming more inner, more special, more subtle than the novel which gave information was.

HOWES. Do you see any informational function in your novels?

KNOWLES. I don't think of that when I'm writing them. James Michener does. He's the best example today.

HOWES. Have your travels and your travel pieces for *Holiday* had any effect on the way you write your novels?

KNOWLES. In *Morning in Antibes* I was obsessed—and that's not too strong a word—with the atmosphere of the Riviera at the time of the Algerian revolt.

HOWES. Is there any "informational" element in the picture of Devon in *A Separate Peace?*

KNOWLES. Yes, by accident *A Separate Peace* is informational about the life of adolescents in World War II. Information is not necessarily separate from the other parts of a novel.

HOWES. Do you think extensive traveling helps the writer to fill in the "informational" side of a novel?

KNOWLES. You don't have to have been there. Thornton Wilder never went to Peru and yet he wrote *The Bridge of San Luis Rey*. On the other hand, I have lived in Lebanon and Greece, but it would be difficult for me to use those settings meaningfully, because I don't know them well enough. Henry James says that a "young lady living in a village" could write about military life, "imagination assisting."[2] But I myself want to have strong feelings about place and be deeply involved in the setting for any fiction I write.

HOWES. You spoke earlier of the contemporary "crisis in the novel." Do you think the novel has a future?

KNOWLES. I think the novel has a rich and long future and people who talk about the death of the novel are just talking hot air. It comes from the literary con men who infest our scene, the nonwriters. It comes from those who can't write but know how to make a living out of other people's work. As long as we want deep inner knowledge of others' lives, the novel, or a form very similar, will endure. TV or McLuhan or the other new rages haven't seriously affected the life of the novel so far. The novel is able to convey a deep inner knowledge of others' lives in a unique way that film and poetry can't do. Characters like Anna Karenina, Emma Bovary, Phineas and Gene—film can't do it. There have been some good film portrayals—Garbo and Vivien Leigh of Anna Karenina, for example—but it's the palest shadow of what we get in the novel.

HOWES. Because the novelist isn't present in the film?

KNOWLES. Yes. You can't do the shadings . . . unless you have, perhaps, a public reading of a novel.

HOWES. I was also thinking of the novelist's special point of view. It seems to me that may be untranslatable into film.

KNOWLES. That's true. The other media are more anonymous.

HOWES. And I suppose that accounts for part of our pleasure in the novel.

KNOWLES. Yes, it's inescapable.

HOWES. Do you have any comments on your present plans?

KNOWLES. I'm writing a novel—*The Paragon*—and I'm half way through, but I wouldn't be able to comment on work in progress. Writing a novel is like peeling an onion, reaching successive layers of significance. And writing one novel leads to the writing of another. Once it's completed you say, "Yes, but I didn't do this or that. . . ." Once you've successfully dealt with something, then you say, "Yes, but there are other problems, other kinds of people I would like to show." Most novelists sooner or later run out of material. I haven't yet.

HOWES. Do you think novelists are more apt to run out of material today than they used to be?

KNOWLES. Yes, most people think they have to write very mean-

2. The reference is to *The Art of Fiction*.

ingful novels. Sinclair Lewis was the last serious novelist who could write his labor novel, his doctor novel, his religious novel, his businessman novel, and so on. It's just like a journalist who would feel he could do something in all different fields—now this has been handed over almost completely to journalists. Today the novel is becoming more inner.

HOWES. And I suppose that may create a problem for younger readers. For example, how would Phineas read *A Separate Peace?* Would he understand and enjoy it?

KNOWLES. Well, I haven't thought about that. What do you think? I don't think he'd really understand it—or want to understand it.

HOWES. He doesn't want to understand because he's hurt by understanding, isn't he?

KNOWLES. Yes. He'd find some of the early parts amusing. Finny sees himself clearly, but he doesn't see others clearly and he doesn't want to. He creates the world he wants to—it's Camelot, isn't it?—and it's destroyed . . . or rather he is.

Two Other Huckleberry Finns

The selection below includes the last two chapters of John Seelye's *The True Adventures of Huckleberry Finn.* Seelye retells Twain's story, often utilizing Twain's own words; but he attempts to meet some of the objections of critics, especially to the last part of the book, and to provide a more natural diction free of "Victorian prudery."

Prior to the beginning of the selection, the King and the Duke have turned Jim in for the reward. Huck wrestles with his conscience and finally decides not to write the Widow Douglas but rather to steal Jim (cf. *Huckleberry Finn,* Ch. 31).

From *The True Adventures of Huckleberry Finn*

JOHN SEELYE

Well, I slept like a dead man that night, and woke up after the birds did. The sky was heavy and grayish, and even that early the air was so warm that your skin got prickly with sweat if you budged. The sun was trying hard to break through, but all it could manage was a sickly chalky streak along the East, low down, and the rest of the sky was a washed-out lead color, like old flannel. It pressed on you, and even the damn birds felt it, and seemed to chirp no more than they had to, and then without much heart for it. A day like that meant trouble or tornadoes, pap used to say, and it was best to stay in a hole till it was over. But time was a-wasting, so

I crawled out and rummaged up something for breakfast. Then I squatted on the downstream end of the raft to take a dump and figure what to do next.

From where the raft was tied I got a good view of the Louisiana side, for maybe a mile or so down the next bend. There was this little steam-sawmill on the bank there, where they had wood stacked and a landing. That seemed a likely spot to start soundings for the place where they had got Jim locked up. I didn't have no real plan. I reckoned one would come along when I needed it.

So I put on my store clothes, and tied up a few traps in a bundle, and took the canoe and cleared for the mill. There warn't nobody about, but it didn't matter none, because painted right across the front was "Phelps Wood Yard," so as to let the steamboats see it, and I knowed I was somewheres near the farm where they had Jim. About a half mile further down there was a clump of cottonwoods running out into the easy water, and I figured to run in there and hide the canoe whilst I poked around a bit. But I hadn't no more'n cleared the mill before there come a power of whooping and hollering from the shore, gunshots and dogs barking to beat hell. I dug out for the channel, not wanting anybody to see me using around there just then. But that was a mistake.

Because when I was already a hundred yards out somebody come a-crashing through the willow thickets—and I see it was Jim! He was all bloody and his clothes was tore up awful. They had been pushing him hard, and he was all weighted down with chains, too. He took one wild look around and seen me out in the river. He didn't say a word, he didn't even wave, he just charged ahead like he was a-going to run all the way, right off the cut bank. It was more'n fifteen feet high there, a reglar bluff, and he went down like a goddamn stone. I thought he was a goner, sure, but I turned the canoe around anyway and come a-booming back in; I hadn't gone very far when a crowd of men and dogs come busting out of the thicket, everybody yelling and howling at once, making powwow enough for a million. It was just like a bear-hunt, only Jim was the bear.

"There he goes!" somebody yelled, and I thought they meant me, only sure enough, there was Jim a-coming on as best he could with all them chains on. A couple of men begun to fire and load, only it's hard to hit a mark in the water, and the bullets didn't come nowheres near to Jim, but went a-whizzing past me with a funny little whispery sound that once you hear it you damn well don't ever forget.

But then a big-assed man with a broadbrim straw and a red goatee held up his hand and hollered: "Hold your fire, goddamn it! That nigger hain't wuth a Continental, dead!"

I figured the man was Mr. Phelps, because that's the way it always is. The people most anxious to shoot a nigger that ain't done just right is always the ones which ain't got any money tied up in him, whilst the man who's got an interest in that nigger, why he's more careful about the nigger's health than his own.

All this time poor Jim kept on a-humping through the water towards me, with only his head showing on account of the chains. He had that worried look a dog gets in the water, and I knew he was having trouble with all that iron on him. But I had to let up paddling because them rips on the bank seemed particularly anxious to shoot somebody, it didn't much matter who.

"You, boy!" Phelps shouted. "Stop that nigger!" He begun to jog along the top of the bank so as to keep up with me and Jim, but warn't having an easy time of it because of the brush growing there. Him and most of the others was fairly awash with sweat, and their clothes was black and limp. Some had throwed themselves down on the bank and was passing a jug around, watching another man who was running around trying to get the dogs together. But they was having such a good time scampering back and forth barking at the place where Jim had jumped off that they paid him no heed. You could see it made him mad, and when the men with the jug begun to poke fun at him and laugh, he got so riled up he hauled back and kicked one of his own hounds right off the bank into the water. It was an ornery thing to do. There ain't no harm in a hound, only sometimes they get so excited they can't hear nothing but their own barking and howling.

I says to Phelps, polite as pie:

"I'd like to help you sir, but I'm only a boy, and that nigger is a full-grown man."

"Well, bring that goddamn canoe in here and *I'll* stop him!"

"There ain't no place," I says, and that was the plain truth. The bank was so high along there that you couldn't a beached a danged scow, let alone a canoe. Just then Phelps run whack into a clump of willows and knocked off his hat. I seen then he was bald as an egg, except where there was a little turf around his ears and the back of his head. It was black, like his eyebrows, which was thick and bushy and run in a straight line across, which is always a sign of meanness, you know.

All above that line was bone white, and below was red as a turkey where he had been sun-burnt. He was glistening so with sweat it looked as though somebody had varnished him.

He says:

"Listen, boy. You see that cave-in about fifty yards down?"

A body would a had to been blind not to, so I said I did.

"Well, you head right for it, and I'll cut around and meet you there."

There warn't anything else I could do that I could see, so I said I would, and he and his men cut back from the bank, where there was less brush. Jim was getting close now, and I could hear him groan whenever he could get his head up to take in air. The rest of the time all you could see was his wool and his eyes, which was all bloody whites, bobbing back and forth. He was having to use most his strength just staying afloat. It was awful to see, but I give him as good a smile as I could work up, the sort of weakly thing you put on when somebody is in their last sickness, and you knowed it and they knowed it, but nobody will let on anybody knowed it.

I looked ahead to the caved-in place, which was getting closer all the time, and I see that the cottonwoods on that little point of land was just a bit further down, and that if Jim and me could get past that point, we'd be clear, because nobody on the bank would be able to see us through them trees.

So now I had a plan, or leastwise half a plan, and the other half come to me in a flash. It was for all the world like one of those puzzles, where all you got to do is figure out where one piece goes and all the rest simply finds their own way.

Phelps and his crew come out of the thickets just then, and I swung the bow round as if to make a run in. The old man he begun to clamber down towards the water, half-sliding in the greasy muck. He had his gun with him, and was holding it out with one hand, so there was only the other free to help himself with, and being so fat and all when he was about half-way down he fell right on his ass and slid to the waters edge, a-cussing to beat hell as he went.

I got up and moved towards the stern end of the canoe, like I was about to get the forrard end high so's to beach it. But then I made as if to stumble, letting go the paddle so it would fall in the river downstream and out of reach. Phelps seen it all.

"Jesus H. Christ! What did you do that fer?"

I begun to rip and carry on, and told him I couldn't swim and would drown for sure and it was all his fault.

"Hain't you got but one friggin' paddle?"

I shook my head, but that was a lie. The other paddle was snuggled down under the front seat, and all the time we was getting closer to the cottonwoods.

The drift was keeping Jim in line with the canoe, but I see he was pretty much played out. He warn't pulling ahead any more, just struggling to keep his head out of the water. But if he could only keep afloat a while longer, everything would be all right. Even if I couldn't pull him in, he could grab a-holt of the stern, and I could clear for the Mississippi side. It was wide down there, more'n a mile across, and there was considerable hiding places—creeks and backwaters and such. They wouldn't ever find us. Once it come on dark we would strike out for the island where the raft was hid, cut her loose, and be fifty miles downstream before daylight. Then I could hunt up a hammer and cold chisel somewhere, and we'd get Jim out of them damn chains for good and all.

Old Phelps was still down in the cave-in, having one hell of a time trying to get back up on the bank, like a red ant caught in a doodle-bug hole. One of his men crept down to give him a hand, but when Phelps took holt of it, he give such a tug that the man come a-tumbling down with him. Somebody had fetched along a rope, like they always do when they go nigger hunting, and next they got it around Phelps and begun to haul him out. He warn't no lightweight, and it took considerable hauling. About the time he was reaching out for the top of the bank, some of the men noticed a steamboat coming up the channel and let out a holler, which the rest joined in with, firing off their guns and jumping up and down, making a power of noise so as to get the pilot's attention. That left only one man on the rope, so down Phelps went to the bottom, leaving the man cussing and spitting on his burned hands.

Well, the pilot seen them, and even give a couple blasts with his whistle, but he kept on a-chunking upstream, most likely figuring they was a bunch of drunks and rowdies, wanting to get on board at the sawmill landing.

By now I was nearly to the cottonwoods, but I had been spending so much time looking back that I only then see what I should a seen before, that them trees was on a sandspit built up by the water from a big creek that emptied in right there, and if I didn't buckle to my paddle right away, the current would take me where I didn't want to go. I fairly bent that paddle, and got through the wash and in towards the easy water by the bank, but when I turned around and looked for Jim, he was already fifty yeards out. Well, I'd druther not have old Phelps see me pull Jim into the canoe whilst we still had less than a gunshot betwixt us, but I didn't have any choice. Besides, the way the current come a-booming out of that creek mouth, there was a good chance we'd be pretty far out before I caught up with Jim.

Well, I laid into the paddle again, and went shooting out into the river. It warn't a minute before a ball went whizzing past and then I heard a pop from the shore, and then two or three more whistled by, and there came a popping like it was Fourth of July. The creek was still carrying me, so I just lay down in the bottom of the canoe, knowing my only chance was to stay low. A couple of bullets thunked into the wood, but it was two-inch thick cypress and I couldn't a been safer if I'd been behind a stone wall.

I could feel the canoe swing this way and that, till she worked free of the cross-currents, and then she swung south and held steady. The shooting had stopped, so I poked my head up and looked around. Phelps's sawmill was out of sight now, behind the spit with the cottonwoods, so I sat up and looked for Jim. I couldn't see him nowheres, and my heart flopped up into my mouth. Next I stood up, bracing myself with the paddle I was a-shaking so but it warn't no use. There was nothing on that whole broad river but me, and I knowed then there warn't no sense looking further for Jim, because he was somewhere deep down under, weighted by them goddamn heavy chains.

Well, I knowed it wouldn't do no good to cry, because all the crying in the world won't bring a dead man alive, but I couldn't help blubbering a little anyhow. For Jim *was* the best cretur, and he was the only true friend I had, even though he was a nigger, and a runaway, too. I guess I didn't rightly know how much he meant to me till he was gone, and I remembered all the good times we'd had on the river, and how fine everything had been up to when them two thieving sons-a-bitches come along and ruined it all.

But now he was gone, just as if he hadn't ever been alive, not even leaving something behind to bury or mourn over, which is a nigger's worst fear, because then he's sure to come back and ha'nt the places where he was happiest, and groan and carry on so because he can't come back, never, except as a ghost, and then only at midnight when everybody is gone or asleep. If I'd knowed where Jim had sank, I would a fetched one of them nigger preachers out to pray over his remainders, but it warn't no use, because the current would carry him somewheres else, downstream, till he caught on a snag maybe. There warn't no use in doing anything, because cannon wouldn't bring him up, nor quicksilver in bread, nor prayer, nor cussing, nor crying. Jim was gone forever, down deep in that old muddy river.

I had left off crying for a spell, and was just lying in the bottom of the canoe thinking these thoughts, when blump! she runs into some willows hanging down from a bank, and a little shower of tiny leaves come tickling down over me. I sat up then and pulled the canoe in under the willows where there was a kind of cave, cool and dark, and I laid back down and tried to think of what I should do next, but it warn't no good. Nothing would come.

It warn't only that I felt low-down and miserable because Jim was dead, that warn't the half of it. Because my conscience begun to work on me, and told me it was all my fault that Jim was dead, and if I had only listened to it before, and done what it said to do, he'd still be alive. It warn't no good blaming the King and the Duke, because they was sent by Providence to trouble us so we'd do right, along with the snakeskin, and the fog, and the rest. For that's always His way, to toss evil in a man's path so he'll do good, and if a body don't pay heed to a little nudge, why Providence'll kick him ass over teakettle next trip around. It's His way, every time.

First He sets your conscience a-picking at you, and if that don't do it, He'll send you a little misery, like a blister, maybe, or a hole in your pocket so you lose something you're particular fond of, or snarl your trot-lines, and if you still don't mend your ways, He'll knock you all kersmash. A body can put up with a talky conscience, but once Providence has it in for him, goodbye! After that, you ain't got no show at all, and only a mullet-head like me will try his luck and stay in the game for another hand. Providence was in it from the very start, and there warn't a damned thing we could a done about it. I suppose I should a been grateful to Him for drownding poor Jim instead of me, but I warn't. It was ornery and wicked, and I knowed it, but I didn't even try. That's how bad I felt, right down to the soles of my feet.

All around it was still and Sunday-like, with everything hot and gray. Gray sky, gray water, everything seemed to have had the color squoze right out of it. The air was full of them kind of faint dronings of bugs and flies that make it seem so lonesome and like everybody's dead and gone, like the sound a spinning wheel makes, wailing along up and sinking along down again; and that *is* the lonesomest sound in the whole world. When a breeze would come along and quiver the willow leaves it made me feel mournful, because it was like spirits whispering—spirits that's been dead ever so many years, or them that's just died. It made me wish I was dead too, and done with it all, and pretty soon I started in blubbering again, and I kept it up off and on until I fell asleep.

Next thing I knowed I woke up with a start, and there was a boom-booming outside on the river like they had got cannon out to raise Jim, but it warn't, it was the storm coming on. The wind swished through the willows something fierce, and I pulled back in as far as I could go. The river was all whitecaps in a flash, foam a-blowing in a line straight as any ruler could make, and then there come a monstrous clap of thunder overhead, and another, and the lighting split everything wide open. The rain come then. It beat down like hailstones, and steam rose up from the river so you couldn't see a thing, just a solid damn sheet of white. The water come trickling through the willows, so I unrolled my blanket and covered up, lying there and listening to the thunder and the swoosh of the rain until I went asleep again. I dreamt then, bad dreams, but I won't tell you what they was about. I already told you.

When I waked up again it was dark night, and the rain had stopped. Leastwise it had stopped outside, but it kept a-dripping down around me through the willows. My blanket was soaked, and my clothes, and the skeeters had sat down on me for dinner, so I figured I might as well get moving once again, and pushed out from under the willows. It took me an hour or two, but I found the little island where I had the raft hid, and clumb aboard. I didn't stay long. I tossed what I wanted into a sack and put it and the gun into the canoe, and the rest I left for anybody that wanted it. Just before I shoved off, I took a last look around to make sure I hadn't forgot anything, and the sight of that lonely raft, all shadows and emptiness, sent a dern lump into my throat like somebody had hit me there. I got into the canoe and never once looked back.

I scrummaged a meal out of some scraps and then I lay down in the canoe with my pipe and thought over what I was to do next. Money warn't no problem, because I still had that yaller boy left in my pocket, and the canoe was worth ten dollars any day. I thought maybe I would go on down to Orleans and ship as a cabin boy on one of the big riverboats. Or maybe head out for the Territory all by myself. I didn't give much of a damn either way. When there's nothing you want to do, or got to do, why you can do anything, but there ain't much joy in it.

Tom Sawyer, now, I knew he'd give his right arm to be me, and to be able to come back to St. Petersburg from the dead, and have Aunt Polly and Becky Thatcher a-weeping over him and maybe have a big parade up to the jail and then a showy trial before they took him out with a brass band to hang him for helping a nigger escape instead of being killed by that nigger and properly dead. Oh, Tom could do it up bully, but somehow I didn't much cotton to the idea. Besides, most likely pap would get a-holt of me again, or even worse the widow, who'd start in sivilizing me all over again, and I couldn't a stood it. I been there before.

It was monstrous quiet out on the river that time of night, and some-wheres far off there was a church bell ringing, but you couldn't hear all the strikes, only a slow *bung . . . bung . . .* and then the next one would drift away before it was finished and there would be nothing for what should been a couple of strikes, and then you could hear *bung . . . bung,* again, and then nothing. At that time of night all the sounds are late sounds, and the air has a late feel, and a late smell, too. All around you can hear the river, sighing and gurgling and groaning like a hundred drownding men, and laying there in that awful dark, I could hear the river terrible clear, and it seemed to me like I was floating in a damn graveyard.

Being out there all alone at that time of night is the lonesomest a body can be. The stars seem miles and miles away, like the lights of houses in a valley when somebody stops on a hill to look back before going on down the road, leaving them all behind forever; and my soul sucked up whatever spark of brashness and gayness I had managed to strike up since that afternoon, and then all the miserableness come back, worse than ever before. But dark as it was and lonesome as it was, I didn't have no wish for daylight to come. In fact, I didn't much care if the goddamn sun never come up again.

•   •   •

In the excerpt below, from Hugo Butler's screenplay for *Huckleberry Finn,* Huck has confided in Captain Brandy, an abolitionist, who has agreed to save the Wilks girls from the King and the Duke and then take Jim upriver on his boat to freedom. When Huck tells Jim these plans, Jim tells him about Pap Finn's death and Huck becomes very angry with Jim for waiting until now to tell him. Huck starts to leave Jim just as a posse, led by the King and the Duke (who know Jim is a runaway slave and that he is wanted for murder), comes tracking Huck and Jim with dogs. The two start running, reconciled for the moment in their mutual danger.

From the Screenplay
for *Huckleberry Finn* (1938)

HUGO BUTLER

CLOSE SHOT — HUCK AND JIM — MOVING CAMERA
Huck strains for all the speed he can make. Jim runs close behind his flying heels.
    HUCK. Got to—find a stream! We gotta find a stream!
He sets his jaw and strains ahead . . . .

FULL SHOT — END OF CORN-FIELD
The dogs, noses to the ground, burst into the open. Unerringly they turn, as Huck and Jim have turned, head down the field. The men break into the open close behind them—follow the dogs. One man stops—lifts a gun and sights it. OVER SHOT *comes the* crack *of a shot.*

MEDIUM SHOT — NEAR GROVE OF SAPLINGS
Huck and Jim dive into the thicket—crash through to the other side.

FULL SHOT — FIELD AT EDGE OF SAPLING GROVE
As Jim and Huck pause for one second on the edge of the grove. Ahead of them is a small, reed fringed pool. It reflects the sharp light of the moon. Huck plunges forward—splashes through the ankle-deep water. Jim follows him to the other side. They gain the hard ground—leap away. CAMERA HOLDS — *the hounds, their baying louder—shoot out of the trees. They follow the trail inexorably—as far as the water. They lose it—course back and forth.*

CLOSE SHOT — JIM AND HUCK
They run desperately—their faces strained—their mouths gasping for air.

Huck stumbles, Jim catches him. They run on.
HUCK. *(sobbing for breath).* That stream—Jim!

FULL SHOT — PART OF A FOREST OF SMALL TREES
In the foreground is the bright ribbon of a small stream. Jim plunges into it—Huck follows. OVER SHOT the baying of the hounds is nearer. Jim splashes down the water-course. Huck follows . . . they round a bend in the stream—disappear. CAMERA HOLDS as the hounds lope to the edge of the water—start to run up and down the bank . . . The Duke and another man break out of the woods and run to the stream . . . Heaving for breath they stand and watch the puzzled hounds. . . .

MEDIUM SHOT — A BREAK IN THE RIVER BANK
Huck and Jim break through the fringe of trees that overhang the end of the stream . . . Huck is leading. He pauses, motions Jim to keep quiet. The baying of the hounds is growing fainter. . . .
HUCK. They've gone the other way! *(triumphantly)* All we have to do is walk up river to the raft!
Huck and Jim wade ashore.
JIM. *(exultantly)* We gave 'em de dodge! We beat 'em! Huck, you *still* my frien'!
He turns happily to Huck. Huck looks at him hesitantly. OVER SHOT comes a metallic whirrrrr!

CLOSE SHOT — HUCK'S LEGS AND FEET
Coiled six inches from his right leg is a diamond-back rattler. It strikes.

CLOSE SHOT — HUCK'S FACE
HUCK *(a shriek). Jim!*

MEDIUM SHOT — RIVER BANK
Jim leaps to his aid. Savagely he crashes his feet on something that seems to be writhing around his heels. The dreadful noise stops. In one motion, Jim drops to his knees and pulls out a knife. Huck, his face taut with fear, is sitting on the bank. Jim pulls up huck's trouser-leg—poises the knife . . . .
JIM. Ready—Huck!
Huck braces himself. Jim cuts quickly. Once. Twice. He drops the knife to the ground and bends over to suck the wound . . . CAMERA HOLDS on Huck's face—white—streaked with running sweat. Jim straightens up, takes a handkerchief and ties it tight as he can pull—around Huck's leg—above the cut. Then he gets to his feet—bends over and lifts Huck in his arms. Holding him against his chest—he hurries off. . . .

CLOSE SHOT — HUCK AND JIM — MOVING CAMERA
HUCK. *(desperately).* Jim, do people always die who've been bit by rattlers?
JIM. *(shaking his head).* No, Huck.

HUCK. Where you takin' me?

JIM. I's got to get you to a doctor. Lay quiet!

HUCK. But you can't, Jim—they'll catch you! *(he screams)* Put me down! *(Jim makes no answer. Stolid, inexorable, he bears Huck away from the river)* Jim ! You gotta go free! Put me down! *(and Huck begins to beat at Jim's chest)* Remember your wife! An' Joey! Put me down!

JIM. We gotta get you to a doctor, Huck.

Huck struggles, beats at Jim with all his strength.

HUCK. Jim! Don't! Jim! *(he faints—grows limp in Jim's arms)*

As Jim moves easily across the ground, as the baying of the hounds comes OVER SHOT. . . .

FADE OUT.

FADE IN: FULL SHOT — STREET — WILKS' HOUSE IN B.G. — NIGHT

A crowd of men surges down the street. Most of the men carry pitch-torches, kerosene lamps. The King and the Duke are perched high above the mob—on a rail. They are the only ones who don't seem to be enjoying themselves. Perhaps the fact that they have been tarred and feathered has something to do with this. . . .

THE KING. Gentlemen! Gentlemen! This is barbarity!

MEDIUM SHOT — INT. WILKS' LIVING ROOM

Captain Brandy and Susan are standing at the french doors, looking into the street. OVER SHOT *comes the shouting of the men. . . .*

SUSAN. I do feel sorry for them, Brandy!

CAPTAIN BRANDY. I imagine they feel pretty sorry for themselves at this moment. *(he turns as Mary Jane comes into scene)* How is he?

MARY JANE. *(nodding her head)* The doctor gave him whiskey. He'll be all right now. . . .

SUSAN. I—I think I'll go upstairs—in case I can help . . . *(she starts for the door)*

CAPTAIN BRANDY. *(quietly).* Don't tell Huck about Jim, Susan. It won't do him any good to know why I had to send him back home. . . .

Susan nods her head and leaves . . . Brandy turns to look sadly out the window. . . .

DISSOLVE TO:

CLOSE SHOT — JIM — INT. COURT ROOM

Humbled, beaten, he sits hunched in a chair. His shoulders droop. Sweat is beaded across his forehead.

JIM. *(as though he has repeated this again and again).* I never killed Huck—I loved Huck and he's alive right this minute.

CAMERA PULLS BACK TO FULL SHOT.

The courtroom is filled with townspeople. In the front row are the Widow Douglass and Miss Watson. The judge sits behind his bench, listening to Jim. . . .

JIM. *(continued).* He he'ped me to escape as far as Pikesville—

an' then—an' then . . . *(desperately)* I've tol' you all the res'! . . .
A smart young man springs up in front of the judge's bench.

YOUNG MAN. Your Honor! It is evident that this man's story—
(indicating Jim) —is a trumped up lie! . . . We have heard witness after
witness testify to the character of Huckleberry Finn. *Every one* of these
witnesses has said that in their opinion it is highly improbable—more—
impossible that Huckleberry Finn would have aided and abetted a runaway
slave!

THE JUDGE. *(coolly).* Opinions are of no consequence in this court,
Mister Bartlett!

BARTLETT. This man's tale is a pathetic attempt to stave off the inevitable! Your Honor, I believe we can only reach one decision!
The Widow Douglass rises. . . . She wears black. . . .

THE WIDOW. Your Honor! *(the judge recognizes her)* I feel that this
case—affects my sister and myself more than anyone else . . . We have
decided to give Jim this one—last chance . . . I am asking that you appoint
someone to travel to Pikesville to investigate Jim's story!
*There is a murmur from the courtroom. Jim sinks back in his chair in
relief. . . .*

THE JUDGE. Thank you, Mrs. Douglass—I feel as you do—in the name
of justice, that precaution can certainly do no harm.

THE WIDOW. Thank you, Your Honor.

BARTLETT *(jumping to his feet).* Your Honor, as head of the citizens'
vigilantes committee, I feel it my duty to warn this court that if verdict is
not passed this day—there is a group of citizens in this town who may see
fit to take the law into their own hands!
There is an ugly murmur from the packed courtroom. It swells ominously.

AD LIB. He killed Huck! Why waste time! What're you waitin' for?

THE JUDGE *(pounding his gavel).* Mister Bartlett! You are in contempt!
Your behavior is disgraceful, sir! Furthermore. . . .
*The rest of his speech is smothered by the noise of scraping
feet . . . CAMERA PANS to the courtroom—men are rising—tramping down
the aisle and out—the murmur is growing.*

DISSOLVE TO:

MED. SHOT — INT. BEDROOM — DAY
*There is a fireplace in the room. The bright fire crackles noisily. Outside, the
rain is splattering against the windows. Huck, a tray on his lap, is sitting up
in bed. . . .*

HUCK. *(indicating the silver coffee-pot—the fine china).* Truly, ma'am, I
never did think I'd get to like food—put out this way.

SUSAN *(taking the tray).* How do you mean, Huck?

HUCK. Well, ma'am, I've always liked my vittles sort o' mixed up—like
in a barrel of odds and ends where things get joggled together and the juice
sort of swaps around, and things go better! . . . *(indicating the tray)* But
that breakfus' was awful good! *(as Susan sets the tray down—causes the
salt-cellar to topple over)* Oh—be careful! . . . Spillin' salt's one o' the easi-
est ways to get bad luck! . . . Throw some over your shoulder!

SUSAN *(throwing a pinch over her shoulder).* Like this?

HUCK. That's it, ma'am . . . *(starting to count on his fingers)* One—two—three days I been here, bein' sick. I figure Jim mus' be with his family by now! Don't you s'pose?

SUSAN *(uneasily).* Yes—I suppose he is. . . .

HUCK. He's in that ol' free state by now! . . . I'd o' given mos' anythin' to see him meet his wife an' Joey! Joey's his son. *(Susan stirs uncomfortably)* Tell me, ma'am, what'd Jim look like when Cap'n Brandy tol' him he was goin' free? I bet his face was jus' one big smile! Eh?

SUSAN. Yes—he was very pleased. . . .

HUCK *(dreamily).* Good ol' Jim—he was about the bes' fren' anyone ever had!

SUSAN *(sharply).* Don't talk like that!

HUCK *(puzzled).* Why not? Why not talk like that?

SUSAN. Because—*(suddenly).* Well—maybe he wasn't such a good friend to have—maybe he wasn't much good!

HUCK. Jim? What're you talkin' about?

SUSAN. Nobody could be your best friend, who was wanted for murder!

HUCK *(jerking upright).* How'd you know that?

SUSAN. Captain Brandy found it out—

HUCK *(suspicious).* When? How?

SUSAN. When he handed him in! He had to, Huck, when he found out Jim was wanted—he *had* to send him back!

HUCK. Send him back! *(Huck starts to get out of bed)* I've got to get Jim!

Susan pushes him back.

SUSAN. You can't get up!

HUCK. You can't stop me!

SUSAN *(holding him).* I'll call Captain Brandy!

Huck eyes her, sees that she means what she says. He flops back in bed. . . .

HUCK *(gasping).* Water! Get me water!

SUSAN *(holding a glass under his nose).* Here, Huck.

HUCK. Not that! I need *cool* water!

SUSAN *(fearfully).* Just lie still, Huck. I'll get it! I'll get it!

She runs out of the room. Huck jumps up in bed—swings his legs over the side and jumps to the floor. He staggers, his legs wobble. Pulling himself erect he takes a pair of pants and starts to drag them on. . . .

QUICK DISSOLVE TO:

CLOSE SHOT — HUCK — DAY — RAIN

Doggedly, he slogs along a country road. He bends forward against the whipping rain . . . He sets his shoulders, wrinkles up his face, strains with the last ounce of his courage to keep on going—OVER SHOT comes the drumming of hoof-beats. . . .

BRANDY'S VOICE. Huck! Huck Finn!

Huck looks behind, starts to run. He trips, stumbles drunkenly. A horse and buggy overtake him. Captain Brandy jumps down and grabs him by the shoulders. . . .

HUCK (*savagely*). Let go! Le' go of me! *(he struggles to get free).*

CAPTAIN BRANDY (*holding him tightly*). Where were you going, Huck, to Jim?

HUCK. *Let me go!*

CAPTAIN BRANDY. Don't, Huck. Don't break your heart . . . Not for Jim. . . He's bad, Huck. He's being tried for murder!

HUCK. He's bein' tried for murderin' me! An' I'm alive hain't I? Jim couldn't murder anybody! He hain't made that way!

CAPTAIN BRANDY. Then they'll give him a chance to prove it! He'll be treated justly. . . .

HUCK (*hysterically*). He's a slave! They'll kill him! They nearly killed him before! I got to get to him!

CAPTAIN BRANDY. You can't do it this way! The road's flooded upriver!

HUCK. I'll get there anyway! Ther hain't no flood can stop me!

CAPTAIN BRANDY (*decisively*). I'll take you, Huck! On the Water Moccasin!

HUCK. Will you, Cap'n Brandy? Will you believe me? Please!

CAPTAIN BRANDY. I believe you, Huck.

For a second they look at each other . . . then Captain Brandy starts to help Huck into the buggy. . . .

DISSOLVE TO:

LONG SHOT — THE WATER MOCCASIN — DAY

Black smoke pouring from her smoke-stacks, she drives upstream. . . .

DISSOLVE TO:

MED. SHOT — INT. PILOT-HOUSE

A lean, weather-beaten man stands at the huge teakwheel. Captain Brandy stands beside him, looking up river. Huck sits on one of the seats, blankets wrapped around him, watching tensely. OVER SHOT *comes the drumming of the engines. The pilot-house itself seems to be vibrating with every turn of the paddle-wheels. The pilot-house door opens and a powerful man enters. He is streaked with soot and sweat. . . .*

MAN (*to Captain Brandy*). She's under full pressure, sir.

CAPTAIN BRANDY. Keep her that way!

MAN. Yes, sir. *(he goes out).*

CAPTAIN BRANDY (*to Huck*). We're doing everything we can, Huck.

(Huck nods silently. His fists clench—tensely, he watches every move that the helmsman makes. . . .

DISSOLVE TO:

CLOSE SHOT — INT. CELL — NIGHT

Jim sits with his head in his hands. OVER SHOT *comes the murmur of men's voices. Jim rises and goes to the window. He looks out through the bars.*

HIS ANGLE — STREET

A group of about a dozen men is gathered at the foot of the jail-steps. Every once and again one of them looks toward Jim's window, points it out to a companion. . . .

CLOSE SHOT — INT. CELL
Jim whirls from the window and paces to the door. A chubby, cheerful-looking little man is opening the door. He carries a plate of food. . . .
> JIM. What those men doin' out there?
> MAN. Oh, probably jus' curious. *(putting the plate of food down).*
> JIM *(shaking his head).* I—I don't like them bein' there. They hain't been there before!
> MAN *(going out).* Don't worry—it don't mean nothin'. Even if it did, we'd take care o' you.
He nods cheerfully and leaves, locking the door. Jim looks after him dumbly. Fearful, puzzled, he turns to look out the window. . . .

CUT TO:

MED. SHOT — INT. PILOT-HOUSE — NIGHT
The pilot, Captain Brandy and Huck bulk large and black in the uncertain light of a swaying kerosene lamp. A white-coated Texas-tender comes into the pilot-house with a tray. He holds it in front of Huck . . . Huck shakes his head.
> CAPTAIN BRANDY. You eat something, Huck . . . .
> HUCK *(hardly aware of what he's doing).* Yes, sir. *(he takes a glass of milk).*
The Texas-tender holds the tray in front of Captain Brandy. He takes a sandwich, hands one to the pilot . . . .
> CAPTAIN BRANDY *(to the pilot).* How does she feel, Tom?
> PILOT *(shaking his head).* River's risin'! We ain't making' what we should!

CLOSE SHOT — HUCK
He sets down the glass of milk. His face is strained. He gets up—shakes the blanket from his feet and goes outside.

MED. SHOT — PILOT-HOUSE
Captain Brandy watches him as he goes out the door.
> CAPTAIN BRANDY *(as the door closes).* Poor kid!
The pilot nods sympathetically. . . .

MED. SHOT — EXT. PILOT-HOUSE NEAR RAIL
There's a watery moon in the sky, and Huck stands at the rail—against the path of the moon. He's looking upriver. OVER SHOT comes the loud thrashing of the paddle-wheels.
> HUCK *(looking down at the river).* You remember Jim—I know you remember him 'cause you've he'ped him before . . . Well, you got to he'p him tonight . . . Jus' 'cause you're big and hain't got no right to be

mean . . . You got to he'p him! . . . An'—an' if you don't—I won't never
pull a skiff on you no more. I won't never swim in you no more. I won't
never see you! . . . Unless you he'p Jim!

CUT TO:

CLOSE SHOT — INT. CELL
*Jim is slumped on his bunk. The plate of food is still on the floor, untouched.
A rock strikes the bars on Jim's window. He sits erect. He gets to his feet and
jumps to the window.*

HIS ANGLE — STREET
*The group of men has swollen to a crowd of twenty or thirty. The crowd is
restless. Suddenly men stoop down, pick up rocks and hurl them at Jim's
window. . . .*
    AD LIB. There he is! That's him! We want him!

CLOSE SHOT — INTERIOR CELL
*Jim falls back from the window—goes to the door and looks down the
corridor. . . .*

CLOSEUP — JIM
Perspiration glistens on his brow.
    JIM *(quietly).* Huck, boy. Where are you?

CUT TO:

LONG SHOT — THE WATER MOCCASIN
*She pounds upstream in the light of the moon. Sparks fly from her smoke-
stacks, a red glow comes from her midship section. . . .*

FULL SHOT — BOILER ROOM
*Five stokers are working desperately. They bang the furnace doors wide—hurl
in great chunks of cordwood—bang the doors shut. The engineer goes from
one to the other, slapping them on the shoulders encouragingly. . . .*
    ENGINEER. Stoke her, boys! *(smiling grimly)* See if you can blow her up!

MED. SHOT — INT. PILOT-HOUSE
As the door opens and Huck comes in.
    CAPTAIN BRANDY *(putting his arm over Huck's shoulders).* We're making
good time, Huck. . . .
    HUCK *(nodding).* We're just passin' Barker's plantation . . . *(to the pilot)*
You can bring her in close to shore here! Make better time—there's no
current and it's good and deep!
    BRANDY. Take her in closer!
    PILOT. We're in too close now!
Reluctantly the pilot swings the wheel. . . .

CUT TO:

CLOSE SHOT — INT. CELL
Jim clings to the cell-door. The noise OVER SHOT *is swelling—louder—
louder. The noise of angry men. The noise of a mob. Jim goes to the window—looks out—eyes wide with terror. . . .*

HIS ANGLE — THROUGH BARRED WINDOW
*The crowd has grown to a mob of between fifty and a hundred men. The mob
is swelling toward the jail doors. The scattered yells and shouts rise to a roar.
The jail doors open and a sheriff and a deputy stand in the entrance. . . .*

INT. CELL
Jim turns from the window—putting his hands over his ears. . . .

FULL SHOT — WATER MOCCASIN — HEAD ON
She slides through the water, fifty, thirty, twenty yards from shore. . . .

INT. PILOT-HOUSE
The pilot, sweat streaming from his face, turns to Captain Brandy. . . .
PILOT. I hain't responsible for her, Captain! We're too close!
CAPTAIN BRANDY. Hold her there! *(he looks toward the shoreline)* We're
making better time! . . .
Suddenly the pilot-house creaks and groans—the boat shudders. . . .
PILOT. We've hit!
HUCK. That sand-bar is a good ten foot under water—we'll make it!
CAPTAIN BRANDY. Hold her on full speed ahead!
PILOT. You'll rip her bottom out!
Captain Brandy looks at Huck.
HUCK. She'll make it!
BRANDY *(grimly)*. Full speed ahead!
The boat shudders, shakes. OVER SHOT *comes the wild beating of the
paddle-wheels. . . .*
PILOT. I won't hold her! I'm going to put her astern!
CAPTAIN BRANDY. Hold her!
*The boat shudders, the strained timbers creak and groan. The pilot-house lists
violently—then swings free as the boat comes off on an even keel. Smoothly,
the paddle-wheels take up their steady beat . . . The pilot starts to swing the
wheel. . . .*
CAPTAIN BRANDY. What are you doing?
PILOT. Taking her into deeper water! *(he whirls the wheel).*
CAPTAIN BRANDY. And fight that current! No you aren't! . . . Do you
know this crossing, Huck?
HUCK. Yes, sir!
CAPTAIN BRANDY. Then take her, Huck!
HUCK. Yes sir!
*He jumps to the wheel. The pilot stands aside—as Huck takes the wheel
confidently, sets her in her marks—and holds her there. . . .*

FULL SHOT — WATER MOCCASIN — HEAD ON
She is barely clearing the shore — but making good time. . . .

INT. CELL
Jim goes to the door—strains to look down the corridor. He turns and goes back to the window.

HIS ANGLE — STREET
The mob is surging up the steps. The sheriff and his deputy retreat into the jail, close the big doors. The mob presses against the doors, heaves and strains . . . The doors begin to creak, to crack. With a grinding crash they fall in . . . The mob rolls into the jail house. . . .

INT. CELL
OVER SHOT comes the noise of pounding feet. The sheriff and his deputy come into sight in the corridor. They stop to lock a barred door that separates the corridor from the entrance to the jail. The first of the mob runs into sight. Jim cowers back into the cell. . . .

INT. CORRIDOR — FULL SHOT
The sheriff and his deputy stand in front of Jim's cell—shotguns pointed at the members of the mob who drag and push at the barred door—
    SHERIFF. I'll shoot I tell you! I'll shoot!
    AD LIB. Go on, shoot! Shoot, and you'll get the same as he gets! Give us the keys!

CLOSE SHOT — JIM
He is cowering in the corner of his cell. Slowly, he straightens up, moves to the front of his cell. His chin is up—his shoulders are square . . . OVER SHOT comes the crash of the door as it falls. . . .

FULL SHOT — CORRIDOR
The men spew through the narrow entrance. The sheriff fires—over their heads. The deputy fires—over their heads. The men overpower the sheriff—take his keys. . . .

MED. SHOT — STREET — FRINGE OF MOB
Huck and Captain Brandy run into scene. Brandy has a pistol. They throw themselves at the stubbornly packed men.
    HUCK. It's me—Huck Finn! It's me—Huck Finn!
Two or three of the men turn, recognize Huck and fall back. . . .

FULL SHOT — INT. CORRIDOR
The men are so tightly packed against the cell door that the man with the keys has some trouble opening the door. Finally he has it unlocked, starts to pull it open. . . .

MAN. Here he is! *Get him!*

HUCK'S VOICE. *Wait! It's me! It's Huck Finn!*

The mob parts—Huck and Captain Brandy walk between the two rows of men. Huck's face is grim—set. . . .

HUCK. *Jim! Jim!*

INT. CELL

Jim hears Huck's voice. He gets up—stumbles to the door. He sees Huck.

JIM *(hysterically)*. Huck!

He breaks down, sobs. Huck puts his arms around him.

WIPE TO:

MED. SHOT — STEPS OF JAIL

Captain Brandy, Huck and Jim come to the door. The mob is frozen in silence. There is no yelling, no movement. Huck goes to the head of the stairs—looks at the men silently . . . finally. . . .

HUCK. When you go home tonight—sit down an' think what the rest o' your life would o' been like—if Cap'n Brandy an' me had got here a little later! *He starts down the stairs—Jim and Brandy follow him. . . .*

DISSOLVE TO:

INT. WIDOW DOUGLASS' LIVING ROOM

Huck stands in front of the Widow with his hat in his hands. The Widow is dabbing at her eyes with a little white handkerchief. Miss Watson and Captain Brandy stand nearby.

HUCK.—so that's how it was, m'am.

THE WIDOW. And Jim's story was all true?

HUCK. All of it, m'am.

THE WIDOW. Still, he did run away, Huck.

HUCK *(bracing himself)*. Yes, m'am. An' I got somethin' to say—if I can—it's about Jim runnin' away . . . I know you'll probably hate me after I say it—But I've been a long way since I saw you last, m'am. An' the farther I went an' the more human bein's I met—the more I got to feel that no human bein' has a right to own another human bein'. M'am, human bein's make enough mess o' their own lives—without messin' up another party's! Tha's why—I want to ask you to let Jim go free!

The Widow looks at Captain Brandy. They exchange the briefest of smiles.

THE WIDOW *(after a pause)*. Huckleberry, I'll do what you ask—but only on several conditions.

HUCK. Yes, ma'am?

THE WIDOW. That you go to school—that you come home and live in my house—that you stop smoking—*(she looks down at Huck's feet—they are bare)* And that you wear shoes. . . .

HUCK *(making up his mind)*. I promise, m'am.

The Widow holds out her hand. Reluctantly, Huck pulls out his pipe—gives it to her. She takes Huck in her arms.

DISSOLVE TO:

CLOSE SHOT — A PADDLE WHEEL BOX
It has "Water Moccasin" gilded on its red side. OVER SHOT *comes the "ting-a-ling" of a bell.* CAMERA PULLS BACK *to show the wheel thrashing the water.*

MED. SHOT — WHARF
Huck and the Widow stand in front of the paddlewheel box—waving. . . .
    HUCK. Good-bye! Good-bye!
The boat is sliding easily away from the dock. . . .

MED. SHOT — DECK
as the boat pulls into the stream . . . *Jim stands at the rail—waving—waving—*
    JIM. Good-bye, Huck!

CLOSE SHOT — JIM
He is smiling the broadest and best smile in all the world—but big tears are rolling down his cheeks. . . .

CLOSE SHOT — HUCK
He grins happily—blinks to keep the tears from overflowing . . . *He waves.* . . .

MED. SHOT — THE WIDOW AND HUCK
Huck is still waving. . . .
    THE WIDOW *(gently).* I don't think he can see you now, Huck.
    HUCK. No, m'am. *(he pulls out his handkerchief—a corncob falls to the wharf. The Widow looks at him accusingly* . . . *Huck picks up the pipe)*
Positively, m'am, it just happens to be one I forgot about!
He throws it into the water. He and the Widow turn and start to walk up the wharf. Peeking over the edge of Huck's hip-pocket is one of the sweetest looking corncobs that God ever grew in Missouri. . . .
CAMERA MOVES DOWN—*Huck is bare-foot*—CAMERA MOVES DOWN—HOLDS ON—*Huck's boots where they rest on the rough planking of the wharf.* . . .

FADE OUT.

BIBLIOGRAPHY

Students may find it more convenient to use other editions than those listed in the footnotes in this text. As an aid, I have listed below paperback editions of most of the works cited in the text.

Angelou, Maya. *I Know Why the Caged Bird Sings.* New York: Bantam Books, Inc., 1971.

Baldwin, James. *The Fire Next Time.* New York: Dell Publishing Co., Inc., 1964.

————. *Go Tell It on the Mountain.* New York: Dell Publishing Co., Inc., 1965.

Bellow, Saul. *Henderson the Rain King.* New York: Compass Books, The Viking Press, Inc., 1965.

Bontemps, Arna. *Black Thunder.* Boston: Beacon Press, Inc., 1968.

Brown, Claude. *Manchild in the Promised Land.* New York: Signet Books, The New American Library, Inc., 1965.

Chesnutt, Charles W. *The Marrow of Tradition.* Ann Arbor, Mich.: University of Michigan Press, 1969.

Cleaver, Eldridge. *Soul on Ice.* New York: Dell Publishing Co., Inc., 1969.

Clemens, Samuel L. *The Art of Huckleberry Finn.* Incl. a facsimile of the 1st ed. Hamlin Hill and Walter Blair, eds. 2nd ed. San Francisco: Chandler Publishing Co., 1969.

Demby, William. *Beetlecreek.* New York: Avon Books, 1967.

Du Bois, W. E. B. *Darkwater: Voices from Within the Veil.* New York: Schocken Books, Inc., 1969.

————. *The Souls of Black Folk.* New York: Washington Square Press, 1970.

Ellison, Ralph. *Invisible Man.* New York: Signet Books, The New American Library, Inc., 1952.

Forster, E. M. *A Passage to India.* New York: Harvest Books, Harcourt Brace Jovanovich, Inc., 1952.

Franklin, John H. *From Slavery to Freedom: A History of Negro Americans.* 3rd ed. New York: Vintage Books, Random House, Inc., 1969.

Gaines, Ernest J. *Of Love and Dust.* New York: Bantam Books, Inc., 1969.

Griffin, John Howard. *Black Like Me.* New York: Signet Books, The New American Library, Inc., 1961.

Hemingway, Ernest. *A Farewell to Arms.* New York: Bantam Books, Inc., 1954.

Hughes, Langston. *Not Without Laughter.* New York: Collier Books, The Macmillan Company, 1969.

Hurston, Zora N. *Their Eyes Were Watching God.* New York: Premier Books, Fawcett World Library, 1969.

Johnson, James Weldon. *The Autobiography of an Ex-Coloured Man.* New York: Hill & Wang, Inc., 1960.

Joyce, James. *A Portrait of the Artist as a Young Man.* New York: Compass Books, The Viking Press, 1956.

Kelley, William Melvin. *A Different Drummer.* Garden City, N.Y.: Anchor Books, Doubleday & Company, Inc., 1969.

Killens, John Oliver. *And Then We Heard the Thunder.* New York: Paperback Library, 1971.

——. *Black Man's Burden.* New York: Simon & Schuster, Inc., 1970.

Malcolm X and Haley, Alex. *The Autobiography of Malcolm X.* New York: Grove Press, Inc., 1966.

Marshall, Paule. *Brown Girl, Brownstones.* New York: Avon Books, 1970.

McKay, Claude. *Banjo.* New York: Harvest Books, Harcourt Brace Jovanovich, Inc., 1957, 1970.

Orwell, George. *Animal Farm.* New York: Signet Classics, The New American Library, Inc., 1956.

Parks, Gordon. *The Learning Tree.* New York: Crest Books, Fawcett World Library, 1970.

Petry, Ann. *The Street.* New York: Pyramid Books, Pyramid Publications, Inc., 1961.

Schuyler, George S. *Black No More.* New York: Collier Books, The Macmillan Company, 1971.

Scott, William Walter, III. *Hurt, Baby, Hurt.* Ann Arbor, Mich.: New Ghetto Press, Inc., 1970.

Steinbeck, John. *Of Mice and Men* (Novel). New York: Bantam Books, Inc., 1955.

——. *The Pearl.* New York: Bantam Books, Inc., 1948.

Thomas, Piri. *Down These Mean Streets.* New York: Signet Books, The New American Library, Inc., 1968.

Thurman, Wallace. *The Blacker the Berry.* New York: Collier Books, The Macmillan Company, 1970.

Walker, Margaret. *Jubilee.* New York: Bantam Books, Inc., 1967.

Williams, John A. *Sissie.* Garden City, N.Y.: Anchor Books, Doubleday & Company, Inc., 1969.

——. *Sons of Darkness, Sons of Light.* New York: Pocket Books, 1970.

——. *This Is My Country Too.* New York: Signet Books, The New American Library, Inc., 1966.

Wright, Richard. *Black Boy.* New York: Perennial Library, Harper & Row, Publishers, 1966.

——. *Native Son.* New York: Perennial Library, Harper & Row, Publishers, 1966.

Yerby, Frank. *Speak Now.* New York: Dell Publishing Co., Inc., 1970.